In Those Days

In Those Days

Collected Writings
on Arctic History

Book 2
Arctic Crime and Punishment

KENN HARPER

INHABIT
MEDIA

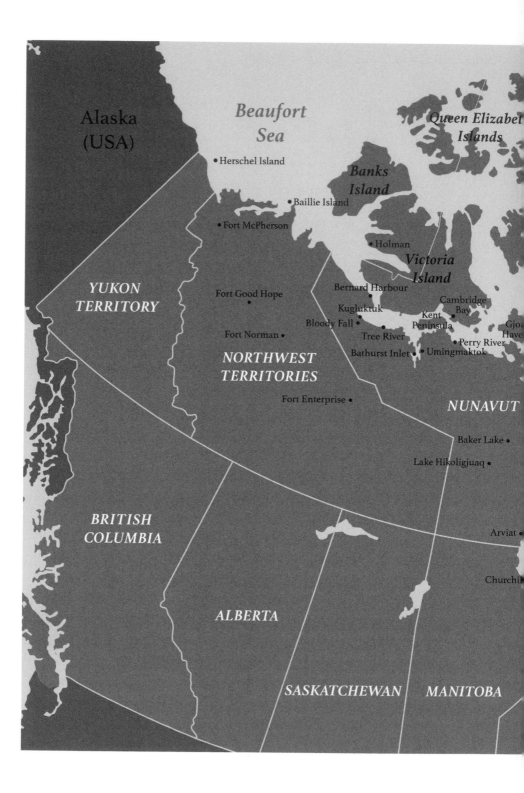

Published by Inhabit Media Inc.
www.inhabitmedia.com

Inhabit Media Inc. (Iqaluit) P.O. Box 11125, Iqaluit, Nunavut, X0A 1H0
(Toronto) 146A Orchard View Blvd., Toronto, Ontario, M4R 1C3

We acknowledge the financial support of the Government of Canada through the
Department of Canadian Heritage Canada Book Fund.

We acknowledge the support of the Canada Council for the Arts for our publishing
program.

Printed in Canada.

Library and Archives Canada Cataloguing in Publication

Harper, Kenn, author
        Arctic crime and punishment / by Kenn Harper.

(In those days: collected writings on Arctic history ; 2)
ISBN 978-1-77227-006-8 (pbk.)

        1. Crime--Canada, Northern--History. 2. Justice, Administration
of--Canada, Northern. 3. Criminals--Canada, Northern--Biography.
I. Title. II. Series: In those days (Series) ; 2

HV9960.C2H37 2015   364.109719   C2015-901172-8

Table of Contents

Introduction

This is the second volume to emanate from a series of weekly articles that I wrote over a ten-year period under the title Taissumani for the Northern newspaper *Nunatsiaq News*. This volume presents stories of crime and punishment in the North. They are stories of real events, involving Inuit and Qallunaat (white people), and the interactions between these two very different cultures. All of the episodes can be documented from the historical record. For some, there is an extensive paper trail; for others, it is scanty. Inuit maintain some of these stories as part of their vibrant oral histories. We need to know these stories for a better understanding of the North today, and the events that made it what it is. They enhance our understanding of Northern people and contribute to our evolving appreciation of our shared history.

I have lived in the Arctic for almost fifty years. My career has been varied; I've been a teacher, businessman, consultant, and

In Those Days

municipal affairs officer. I moved to the Arctic as a young man, and worked for many years in small communities in Qikiqtaaluk (then Baffin) Region—one village had a population of only thirty-four. I also lived for two years in Qaanaaq, a community of five hundred in the remotest part of northern Greenland. Wherever I went, and whatever the job, I immersed myself in Inuktitut, the language of Inuit.

In those wonderful days before television became a staple of Northern life, I visited the elders of the communities. I listened to their stories, talked with them, and heard their perspectives on a way of life that was quickly passing.

I was also a voracious reader on all subjects Northern, and learned the standard histories of the Arctic from the usual sources. But I also sought out the lesser-known books and articles that informed me about Northern people and their stories. In the process I became an avid book collector and writer.

The stories collected in this volume all originally appeared in my column, Taissumani, which I write for *Nunatsiaq News*. Taissumani means "long ago" in Inuktitut. In colloquial English it might be glossed as "in those days," which is the title of this series. The columns appear online as well as in the print edition of the paper. It came as a surprise to me to learn that I have an international readership, which I know because of the comments that readers send me. I say it was a surprise because I initially thought of the columns as being stories for Northerners. No one was writing popular history for a Northern audience, be it native or non-native. I had decided that I would write history that would appeal to, and inform, Northern people. Because of where I have lived and learned, and my knowledge of Inuktitut, these stories would usually (but not always) be about the Inuit North. The fact that readers elsewhere in the world show an interest in these stories is not only personally gratifying to me, but should be satisfying to Northerners as well—the world is interested in the Arctic.

I began writing the series in January 2005. Originally the articles were datelined. I picked an event in the past that could be accurately dated, and wrote a column about it on the anniversary of that date. But I eventually found that formula unduly restrictive. Since shaking off the shackles of the dateline, I have simply written about an event, person, or place that relates to Arctic history. Most deal with northern Canada, but some are set in Alaska, Greenland, or the European North. My definition of the Arctic is loose—it is meant to include, in most of the geographical scope of the articles, the areas where Inuit live, and so this includes the sub-Arctic. Sometimes I stray a little even from those boundaries. I don't like restrictions, and *Nunatsiaq News* has given me free rein to write about what I think will interest its readers.

The stories are presented here substantially as they originally appeared in Taissumani, with the following cautions: Some stories that were presented in two or more parts in the original have been presented here as single stories. For some, the titles have been changed. There have been minimal changes and occasional corrections to the text. I have occasionally changed punctuation in direct quotations, if changing it to a more modern and expected style results in greater clarity.

The chapters have been organized generally in chronological order. They are meant to be read independently.

Qujannamik.
Kenn Harper
Iqaluit, Nunavut

A Note on Word Choice

Inuk is a singular noun. It means, in a general sense, a person. In a specific sense, it also means one person of the group we know as Inuit, the people referred to historically as Eskimos. The plural form is *Inuit*.

A convention, which I follow, is developing that *Inuit* is the adjectival form, whether the modified noun is singular or plural; thus, an Inuit house, Inuit customs, an Inuit man, Inuit hunters.

Some stories refer to Inuit in northwestern Greenland (the Thule District). They refer to themselves in the plural as Inughuit. The singular, *Inughuaq*, is seldom used, *Inuk* being used instead. The adjectival form is *Inughuit*.

The language spoken by Inuit in Canada is Inuktitut, although there are some regional variations to that designation. The dialect spoken in the western Kitikmeot Region is Inuinnaqtun. That spoken in Labrador is called Inuktut. The language spoken by the Inughuit of northwestern Greenland is Inuktun.

In Those Days

The word *Eskimo* is not generally used today in Canada, although it is commonly used in Alaska. I use it if it is appropriate to do so in a historical context, and also in direct quotations. In these contexts, I also use the old (originally French) terms *Esquimau* (singular) and *Esquimaux* (plural).

I have generally used the historical spellings of Inuit names, sometimes because it is unclear what they are meant to be. The few exceptions are those where it is clear what an original misspelling was meant to convey, or where there is a large number of variant spellings.

A Hostage-Taking in the Arctic

It didn't start out as an abduction.

Martin Frobisher set sail from England in 1576 on the first of his three Arctic voyages in command of two vessels, the *Gabriel* and the *Michael*. The voyage was sponsored by the Muscovy Company and its purpose was to find a Northwest Passage to the riches of the Far East. On August 11, the *Gabriel* entered Frobisher Bay. (The *Michael*, which had become separated from the *Gabriel*, had turned back for Britain.)

From an island near the head of the bay, Frobisher and Christopher Hall surveyed the body of water that, despite its progressive narrowing, they thought was the sought-for passage west. Then they spotted objects moving in the water at a distance:

In Those Days

"And being ashore, upon the toppe of a hill," a contemporary account related, "he perceived a number of small things fleeting in the Sea a farre off, whyche he supposed to be Porposes or Ceales, or some kinde of strange fishe: but coming nearer, he discovered them to be men, in small boates made of leather."

Frobisher and his men were about to be part of the first documented encounter between Englishmen and Inuit.

The Englishmen retreated to the safety of the *Gabriel*, while the Inuit made land. Hall then went ashore with the ship's boat, a white flag waving to show his peaceful intent. He invited one Inuk to come to the ship and left one sailor ashore. At this point each side had a hostage. The Inuk was fed and given wine, and when he returned to land he reported that he had been well treated. The English hostage returned to the ship. Nineteen more Inuit arrived and came aboard. They showed no fear of the Englishmen and seemed familiar with ships. It is probable that they had seen Europeans before.

The two groups traded. The Inuit brought fish and meat as well as seal and bear skins, and received in return bells, mirrors, and other trade objects.

Frobisher attempted to hire one of the Inuit men as a pilot to guide him through the passage he thought led to the west. But there was probably a misunderstanding about this on both sides. Five of Frobisher's men were dispatched in the ship's boat to take the man ashore to get his kayak. Instead of putting him ashore in sight of the ship, they rowed around a headland, where three of them went ashore with the man. The boat, with two men in it, was then seen offshore, and Frobisher made signs that they should return to the ship. The boat disappeared again behind the headland, presumably to pick up the other men. Frobisher's five men were never seen by Englishmen again.

A few days later, the man who had been the first to board the ship some days earlier approached the vessel in his kayak, no doubt to trade. He was cautious, but Frobisher lured him close to the ship with a bell. He dropped the bell into the water, but out of reach of the Inuk. Then Frobisher lured him closer by ringing a larger bell over the side of the ship. As the Inuk reached for the bell, Frobisher seized the man's hand, then grasped his wrist with his other hand and lifted the man and his kayak out of the water and onto the deck of the ship in one smooth motion. A chronicler of Frobisher's voyage wrote that the man bit his tongue in two.

Frobisher held the man hostage for a time, hoping to exchange him for his five missing men and his much-needed boat. But the Inuit who came near the ship in their kayaks did not offer up the five men. With the loss of his ship's boat and some of his most able-bodied men, Frobisher gave up his mission. On August 25, with the unfortunate Inuk still on board, he turned sail for England.

The hostage was now a captive and could be used to prove to Queen Elizabeth I that Frobisher had reached a far-off land.

They reached London on October 9, where the Inuk became the talk of the town. George Best described him as "this strange infidel, whose like was never seen, read, nor heard of before, and whose language was neither known nor understood of any."

Unfortunately, this nameless captive did not survive long. He died in London and was buried in St. Olave's Church, a church that still stands near the Tower of London. The church records, however, do not record the burial of the Inuk, and so he remains nameless, the first recorded casualty in a clash of cultures in the Canadian Arctic.

Five
Missing Men

On August 20, 1576, five sailors from Martin Frobisher's ship *Gabriel* went ashore at Frobisher Bay. Five days later, Frobisher gave up hope that the men would return, and set sail for England. Michael Lok, one of the explorer's backers, wrote that Frobisher, having heard nothing of or from the men, "judged they were taken and kept by force."

What happened to those five white men four centuries ago?

The British assumed that they had been captured, held against their will, and probably murdered. But over two centuries later, Inuit oral history told a different tale.

In 1861 Charles Francis Hall, an American exploring in Frobisher Bay, heard a story from an ancient Inuit woman, Uqijjuaqsi (whose name he spelled Ookijoxy). Hall wrote:

Oral history told me that five white men were captured by Innuit people at the time of the appearance of the ships a great many years ago; that these men wintered on shore (whether one, two, three, or more winters, could not say); that they lived among the Innuits; that they afterward built an oomien (large boat), and put a mast into her, and had sails; that early in the season, before much water appeared, they endeavoured to depart; that, in the effort, some froze their hands; but that finally they succeeded in getting into open water, and away they went, which was the last seen or heard of them.

Hall took the story down in haste through a less-than-skilful interpreter, and recognized that there might be some inaccuracies in his account. In the book he wrote about his expedition, he noted, "I have put down here only a part of what I recorded in my journal at the time, and, consequently, much of it will be found to have been the result of some slight mistake in what I then understood."

Talking with Uqijjuaqsi later, this time using the Inuit woman Tookoolito as interpreter, he added to the information he had gleaned about this missing party.

The white men had apparently gotten along well with the Inuit, and especially with one man, whose name Uqijjuaqsi remembered as being "Eloudjuarng." He was, Hall wrote, "a great man or chief among the Inuit. Tookoolito described him as being 'All same as king.'" When the white men were about to set out for home, Eloudjuarng composed a song wishing them a quick and safe passage, "and he caused his people, who were very numerous, to sing it." But the white men failed in their attempt to flee the country, and "finally froze to death."

In Those Days

Robert McGhee[1], an Arctic archaeologist and historian, felt that neither the English assumptions about the men's capture and murder, nor the Inuit belief that they had been accidentally or purposely marooned, seemed entirely plausible. He suggests that the Inuit may well have wanted to steal the ship's boat, wood being a very valuable commodity, but that they would have had no other reason to hold the men hostage. Moreover, the account by Michael Lok does not speak of violence, but rather suggests that the Englishmen may have acted voluntarily.

McGhee suggests this possibility:

Perhaps we should try to imagine the motives of the five sailors, young men who for ten weeks had endured the cramped quarters of a cold, wet, pitching ship. They had lived on bad food and worse beer, and had slept huddled together on the hard deck of the tiny forecastle. They had been subject to the discipline of a captain famous for his temper and impetuous actions. For the past few days they had come to be acquainted with the most extraordinary people they had ever met, smiling strangers who brought them fresh fish . . . dressed in warm furs, [they] were eager to trade furs and ivory objects that could easily be sold for a profit at home in England, and introduced the sailors to their shy, tattooed, and charming wives and daughters. An invitation to come ashore and further their acquaintance, as well as to walk freely on the dry tundra and drink clean water from a stream, may have been too enticing to resist.

McGhee suggests that the sailors may have stayed ashore longer than they intended, and perhaps feared punishment from their volatile commander for disobeying orders. The Inuit, for their part, would have discussed the merits of acquiring the valuable wooden boat. "The fate of the sailors," McGhee wrote, "would have been entirely dependent on the nature of the camp leader. If the traditional Inuit stories are to be believed, the men may have been fortunate in encountering a leader who not only spared their lives but made sure that they survived in the community. However, he may not have possessed the power to have the boat returned to Frobisher's ship, and the subsequent kidnapping of an Inuit man would likely have put an end to any talk of compromise."

McGhee has offered a plausible scenario, but after the passage of over four hundred years, we will never know with any certainty what became of Frobisher's five missing men.

1 I have quoted at length
   from Robert McGhee's writings,
   with his permission.

Henry Hudson's Mutineers and the Inuit

In the summer of 1611, a mutiny occurred on Henry Hudson's ship, the *Discovery*. Having spent a difficult winter in James Bay, members of the crew were concerned about Hudson's secrecy and his seeming desire to loiter in James Bay, searching every bay and river estuary that might lead to a passage to the Pacific. The conspirators cast Hudson, his son John, and seven other men, including those who were sick, adrift in a tiny shallop. The *Discovery* then began its tortuous return to England under the leadership of Henry Greene and Robert Juet.

On July 26 the ship reached Cape Wolstenholme, the north-westernmost tip of present-day Nunavik, where the crew would naturally expect to make a right turn into Hudson Strait. But first there was the matter of food. Their supplies were almost exhausted. In their haste, they had ignored the rich sea-mammal resources of Hudson Bay's east coast. So a detour was made to East Digges Island, where the men knew there was a murre colony. For some of this motley crew, it was a fatal detour.

A shore party of Englishmen encountered a group of Inuit camped on the island, there for the same purpose: to secure a supply of seabirds as food. The two groups made contact. Although there is no record of previous contact between white men and Inuit in this area, the Inuit probably knew about the existence of strangers like these from across the sea. Inuit on Baffin Island had encountered Qallunaat (white people) on the earlier Frobisher expeditions, and those on the Labrador coast had periodic contact with Basque, French, and English fishermen. News of these strangers and their trade goods would have reached Nunavik from one or both of these sources.

The Inuit showed the white men their way of knocking the murres from the cliffs with long poles. The white men demonstrated their method—blasting them out of the air, seven or eight at a time, with a musket shot.

After the visit to the bird cliffs, the two groups got down to the business of trade. The Inuit offered many products of the land and sea, but the English wanted only walrus ivory. They got what they wanted in return for a knife and two glass buttons. By signs, the Inuit told the leader, Henry Greene, that his party should return the next day to barter for fresh meat. Or so Greene thought.

The following day, Greene returned with five men in the ship's boat. They saw the Inuit "dancing and leaping" on the hills as they put in to a sheltered cove. The Inuit rushed forward, anxious to barter. Greene and another man showed off their trade items: bells, mirrors, and a jew's harp. One man clamoured into the ship's boat, where Habakkuk Prickett, a young crew member who had signed on to the voyage as a representative of one of Hudson's main patrons, sat. Prickett, nervous, motioned for him to go ashore. But another Inuk was in the boat and attempted to stab Prickett. Prickett fended off the main thrust of the strike but still sustained wounds to his arm, chest, and thigh. Finally he managed to over-power his assailant and stabbed him in the chest and throat.

Meanwhile, other Inuit had attacked the Englishmen who were ashore. Two were virtually disembowelled. But all made it to the shallop and fled for the *Discovery*, which lay a short distance away. Next the Inuit used their bows and arrows, and shot Henry Greene dead. Another arrow struck Prickett in the back, but he survived. His Inuit attacker and the two men who had been most seriously wounded onshore all died aboard the *Discovery* that very day. Another man died two days later. Of the six men of the shore party, only Prickett and one other man survived.

It is an often-quoted cliché that the winners get to write history. The Inuit must be counted the winners in this inexplicable attack. But the losers wrote the account. Habakkuk Prickett was one of the survivors who reached England in the fall of 1611, and his story is the only recounting we have of this strange episode. He blamed it all on Henry Greene and suggested that "we take heed of the savage people." Whether the attack by the Inuit was unprovoked or the result of a tragic misunderstanding, we will never know.

From East Digges Island the survivors sailed Hudson's ship, the *Discovery*, through Hudson Strait and across the Atlantic to England. Upon their return they had a lot of explaining to do. Mutiny was a serious offence, and the task of this malnourished group of adventurers was to present an alibi that would hold water, if they were to avoid possible death sentences.

One way they did this was to hold out the hope that the route to and through Hudson Bay still held promise for enterprising investors to discover the Northwest Passage, and with it, a route to the riches of the Orient.

Perhaps no one was more adept in this regard than the wily Habakkuk Prickett, supercargo on the expedition. A supercargo was essentially a passenger, not part of a ship's working crew, put aboard as a representative of the investors or of the ship's owners. Prickett represented the interests of Sir Thomas Smythe of the Haberdashers' Company—and that is almost all we know of him.

Prickett's tack in trying to convince the investors that they should back further expeditions to the northwest, despite having just backed one that achieved nothing, centred in part on the attack by the Inuit. More to the point, it centred on the knife that an Inuk had wielded against him with such force that it had come very close to rendering him a corpse. The chronicler Samuel Purchas acquired some of Prickett's papers and wrote in 1625 about the experience of Prickett and his mates and the arguments for a passage through North America to the Pacific. Purchas wrote, "The weapons and arts which they [the mutineers] saw, beyond those of other savages, are arguments hereof. He which assaulted Prickett in the boat, had a weapon broad and sharp indented, of bright steel (such as they use in Java), riveted into a handle of morse [walrus] tooth."

The conclusion that Prickett had, then, tried to convey was that these Inuit had come from the Pacific, or that the knife had come from the Pacific and made its way eastward to be traded through the long-sought passage.

In Those Days

This was a long shot, and there is no record of whether the investors took any heed of it. Nonetheless, the following year the Northwest Company, Hudson's sponsor on his fatal expedition, and the Prince of Wales sent out another expedition in search of the elusive passage.

But Prickett had described a knife very un-Inuit in character. The event had happened in 1611; no ships were known to have traversed Hudson Strait by that date—George Weymouth's 1602 expedition had entered the strait, but only for a short distance. Where had this steel-bladed knife come from?

Of course, there is the possibility that Prickett fabricated his description of the weapon. But if he did not, and the knife was as described, it had certainly not come from the Orient. Probably it had come from the southern reaches of the Labrador coast, where Inuit were known to trade with whalers and fishermen, and been traded from hand to hand up the coast. It also might have come from across Hudson Strait, from the Inuit of Baffin Island. George Best, who left an account of Martin Frobisher's earlier voyages to Frobisher Bay, wrote of the Inuit encountered there that "it appeereth they trade with other nations which dwell farre off." Many modern scholars also suspect that Basque whalers may have whaled as far north as Davis Strait, and with whaling generally comes trade.

No one knows what happened to the knife that tore into Habakkuk Prickett's thigh. Prickett overpowered the Inuk and took him aboard ship, where he died. Presumably Prickett kept the knife. Perhaps it lies today, unidentified, in a museum or a damp British attic, an unknown relic of an attack, the motives for which are still a mystery.

Massacre at Knapp's Bay

T he west coast of Hudson Bay north of Churchill, what we know today as the Kivalliq or Keewatin Region, was largely Chipewyan Indian territory three hundred years ago. The Chipewyans spent their winters in the boreal forest but followed the caribou herds north of the tree line in the summer, possibly right to the Arctic coast. A group of Inuit—probably numbering between one hundred and two hundred—migrated from Coronation Gulf far to the west (the Kugluktuk area) to the vicinity of Chesterfield Inlet between 1650 and 1715. Some scientists surmise that, en route, they spent several generations on an upper arm of the Thelon River, a wooded area. If so, their new coastal home on Hudson Bay would have been a marked change from what they were used to.

The move brought the Inuit onto a coast that was seasonally

In Those Days

Chipewyan territory. (Inuit had lived as far south as Churchill between 1200 and about 1450, but had withdrawn far to the north by 1500 as a result of a deteriorating climate.)

By the early years of the eighteenth century, there was a third group involved in the southern part of this area. In 1717 the Hudson's Bay Company had established a post at Churchill and very quickly established trade relations with the "Northern Indians" and the "Southern Indians," their names for the Chipewyan and the Cree.

The very next year the Company began sending trading vessels north along the coast during the summer, to trade with the Inuit at Whale Cove, and to the south at Knapp's Bay, near present-day Arviat. They wanted to learn more about the potential for trade with the Inuit, and to entice them south to trade at Churchill.

But the Inuit resisted the suggestion, probably in fear of the Chipewyans. Company officials too questioned the policy, writing to London, "We think there may be danger in drawing them to Ascomay Point [Churchill River] . . . while so mortal an enmity is subsisting between them and the Northern Indians." So in 1739 the Bay changed its tactic: it would trade each summer by ship as far north as the ice would permit.

The Chipewyans resented the actions of these two groups of newcomers—the British and the Inuit—in what they viewed as their territory. They saw the British policy as favouritism. The Chipewyans had to travel over great distances to trade at Churchill, while the Inuit had only to remain in their camps and the floating trading posts would come to them.

In 1755, John Bean, captain of the sloop *Churchill*, traded with Inuit at Knapp's Bay and reported them "very kind and courteous." He provided them with awls, needles, files, hatchets, tin pots, and ice chisels, and in return they gave him blubber and baleen, as well as five wolf pelts and two fox skins.

While John Bean had been guiding his ship northward, a group of Chipewyans had been travelling south on foot, bound for Churchill to trade. When they saw the vessel, they sent up a smoke signal, but Bean realized it was a Chipewyan signal and ignored it. His instructions were to trade only with Inuit on the coast. The Chipewyans were incensed. They reversed their course and followed the vessel along the coast to Knapp's Bay. Unseen by the Inuit and the British, they watched the trading until the vessel left. Then they waited until everyone was asleep in their tents, and attacked. They killed between sixteen and eighteen people. They kept one young woman alive, but when she escaped, they tracked her to a shallow pool where she was hiding and "shot her instantly in the water."

Hudson's Bay Company records distinguish between "Home Indians" and "Away Indians." The "Home Indians" lived at or near the trading posts, and the company employed them as interpreters, hunters, and labourers. They learned English and the dialects of any Aboriginal neighbours, and became familiar with company trading methods and policies. "Away Indians" lived far from the posts; they were more traditional hunters, and less familiar with the ways of the white men. The massacre at Knapp's Bay was undoubtedly the work of "Away Indians."

Despite this incident, there was no subsequent increase in hostilities between Chipewyans and Inuit. In fact, the opposite occurred. The "Home Indians" wanted peace, as did the British and the Inuit. A few years after the incident, a few Chipewyan families began to spend their summers alongside the Inuit at Knapp's Bay. They told the captain of a trading vessel in 1762 that there was a truce between the groups. Two years later, a company official reported that the Inuit and Chipewyans were "now tolerably well reconciled with each other."

For the next quarter century, Chipewyans and Inuit lived in peace at Knapp's Bay, an early and successful experiment in biculturalism. The Chipewyans were even the larger of the two groups, often outnumbering the Inuit three to one.

But this cooperation came to a sudden end. And violence had nothing to do with it. A smallpox epidemic in 1781–82 almost wiped out the Chipewyans. The French seized and occupied Churchill between 1782 and 1784, which prevented all trade north. On top of this, the climate was noticeably deteriorating. The Little Ice Age resulted in ocean cooling and terrible ice conditions off the Kivalliq coast. The caribou herds declined, making the area even less hospitable for the few remaining Chipewyans, who left the coast and withdrew to the more southerly forest.

Today, an opposite climate change, global warming, is noticeably affecting Inuit communities throughout the Arctic. Who can predict what changes it will cause to settlement patterns and land use practices that we take for granted today?

Slaughter at Bloody Fall

The names of Samuel Hearne and Matonabbee are inextricably linked in Northern history.

Hearne was born in England in 1745. Orphaned young, he entered the service of the Royal Navy at the age of eleven, later joining the Hudson's Bay Company, which sent him to Churchill in 1766. Moses Norton, in charge of that post, was obsessed with exploiting a copper mine rumoured to exist in the Far North. Chipewyans had brought specimens of the ore to Churchill in 1767, which further whetted Norton's desire to find and exploit the deposit.

Hearne, described as "diligent and trustworthy but not an assertive character," left Churchill on foot in November 1769, with two white servants and a party of Indians, prepared for a journey of up to two years. But the attempt was a disaster and, even before

In Those Days

Christmas, Hearne was back at Churchill. The following year he made another abortive attempt, turning back for Churchill in August. In September, while still making his way back to the post, he met the Chipewyan leader Matonabbee, who was on his way to Churchill to trade. The two reached Churchill together on November 25. Hearne described the man as the "most sociable, kind and sensible Indian I had ever met with."

Matonabbee had been born about 1736 to a "slave woman" whose origins are unknown. She had been a slave to an Indian, who traded her to the Hudson's Bay Company at Churchill. Richard Norton, manager of the post, gave her to a Chipewyan man, and that man became Matonabbee's father. Soon after, both parents were dead and Richard Norton unofficially adopted the boy. When Norton retired in 1741, Matonabbee, still a child, rejoined his Chipewyan relatives. Eleven years later, then in his late teens, he returned to Churchill, where he was hired by the company as a hunter to supply game to the post.

At Churchill, Matonabbee learned the Cree language and "made some progress in English." Hearne thought him punctual, truthful, and "scrupulous." Nearly six feet tall, he was strong, energetic, and courageous. The new manager at Churchill, Ferdinand Jacobs, selected him to make peace between the Chipewyans and their long-standing rivals, the western Cree. Matonabbee worked patiently over many years to bring about peace and establish trade between the two groups. During this period he acquired influence, and at least seven wives.

After Hearne's return from his aborted second journey in search of the copper mine, he spent only twelve days at the trading post before Norton again directed him to take up the search, this time in company with Matonabbee. Hearne's journal makes it quite clear that Matonabbee was in charge. Hearne later wrote of him in endearing terms, describing his "benevolence and universal humanity to all the human race, according to his abilities." This is a remarkable characterization in light of Hearne's knowledge that Matonabbee had murdered one of his spouses for casting doubt on his ability to satisfy seven wives. It is even more remarkable considering the events that happened when the party reached the Coppermine River. Nonetheless, the two men were friends, and both were devoted to the goal of reaching the Coppermine by land.

The party travelled west during the winter, then turned northward in April. At Clowey Lake, Hearne was disillusioned when a large group of western Indians joined their party with the expressed intent of murdering any Inuit that they might encounter at the mouth of the Coppermine. Hearne protested, but to no avail, and eventually gave up, to the point that—amazingly—he wrote in his journal that "I did not care if they rendered the name and race of the Esquimaux extinct."

On July 17, 1771, Hearne's fears were realized when the party surprised a camp of Inuit sleeping in their tents near the mouth of the river. That morning, Hearne's Indian guides killed over twenty Inuit—men, women, and children. Hearne left a heart-wrenching description of the slaughter:

> The shrieks and groans of the poor expiring wretches were truly dreadful; and my horror was much increased at seeing a young girl, seemingly about eighteen years of age, killed so near me, that when the first spear was stuck into her side she fell down at my feet and twisted round my legs, so that it was with difficulty that I could disengage myself from her dying gasps. As two Indian men pursued this unfortunate

In Those Days

victim, I solicited very hard for her life; but the murderers made no reply till they had stuck both their spears through her body and transfixed her to the ground. They then looked me sternly in the face, and began to ridicule me, by asking if I wanted an Esquimaux wife; and paid not the smallest regard to the shrieks and agony of the poor wretch, who was twining round their spears like an eel!

Hearne was unable to prevent the massacre. Matonabbee did not attempt to prevent it, and in fact participated willingly in it. Hearne named the spot Bloody Fall. The name lives in infamy today.

Recent research and comparisons of Hearne's published account with his unpublished journal have led to doubt as to the veracity of the published version, and even to doubt as to whether Hearne was present at the time of the massacre. Nonetheless, this is the account that captured the public interest and endures in the historical record to this day.

Robert Hood

Passion and Murder in the North

In 1819, the British explorer John Franklin set out on his first Arctic land expedition. Its purpose was to explore the northern coast of North America eastward from the mouth of the Coppermine River. In June of 1821, Franklin and his party left Fort Enterprise, the headquarters that they had established at Winter Lake north of Great Slave Lake, and followed the Coppermine River to the Arctic coast, which they reached in mid-July.

The exploration party travelled east in two canoes, charting the coast and naming features in Coronation Gulf, Bathurst Inlet, and Melville Sound. At Kent Peninsula, they turned back at the aptly named Turnagain Point, because of a lack of supplies and the lateness of the season. There was also discontent among the French-Canadian boatmen. They returned overland to Fort Enterprise. The return trip was disastrous. Ten of the boatmen

In Those Days

starved to death, one man was murdered, and another was executed.

The murdered man was Robert Hood, son of a British clergyman. He had joined the Royal Navy as a midshipman at the age of fourteen, and engaged with the Franklin expedition in that capacity when he was twenty-two. Skilled in surveying, mapping, and landscape delineation, he was a valuable member of Franklin's party. A biographer has described him as "conscientious, hardworking, honest, self-effacing, stoical, and possessed of an inquiring, philosophical mind and a wry sense of humour."

On October 7, on the disastrous return trek from the coast, Robert Hood was in a very weakened state. The doctor and naturalist, John Richardson, and a seaman, John Hepburn, camped with him, hoping that he might regain his strength. The other men continued ahead with Franklin. On October 9, one man, an Iroquois voyageur named Michel Terohaute, known in expedition records simply as Michel, returned to Richardson's tent. Two days later, returning from a hunting trip, he brought Richardson and his small group some "wolf meat." They realized only later that it was probably meat from the bodies of two other voyageurs, whom Michel had likely murdered. By the eighteenth Hood was in desperate condition, barely able to sit up. Two days later he and Michel got into a loud argument, which ended when Michel shot the midshipman through the back of the head.

The evidence against Michel was circumstantial. No one had witnessed the killing. Michel protested his innocence, but it was apparent that Hood had not shot himself from the back. Richardson and Hepburn feared that they might become Michel's next victims. On October 22, when Michel returned from another hunting foray, Richardson repaid him for Hood's death by shooting him through the head. An eye for an eye.

Ironically, Hood's short life could have ended much earlier on the expedition, were it not for the keen observations and surreptitious actions of John Hepburn. Decades later, Hepburn told the French explorer Joseph René Bellot that earlier in Franklin's expedition, Hood and another midshipman, George Back, had both fallen in love with a fifteen-year-old Copper Indian girl, Greenstockings. Their rivalry was so intense that they announced their intention to fight a duel over her. Disaster was averted only because Hepburn covertly removed the charges from their pistols.

To separate the two men, Franklin then sent Back off to Fort Chipewyan, eleven hundred miles away, to get supplies. Hood, an accomplished artist, produced a portrait of Greenstockings. Later, after Hood's death, the young woman gave birth to his daughter. Their romance was the subject of Rudy Wiebe's award-winning novel *A Discovery of Strangers*, published in 1994.

Hood was promoted to lieutenant while on the expedition. But by the time word reached Franklin of the advancement, Hood had already been dead for six weeks.

Inuit Evidence in a British Court

John Franklin and the crews of his ships *Erebus* and *Terror* left England in 1845 on the most famous expedition in Arctic history. They never returned.

On May 15, 1845, only five days before the ships departed England, the mate of the *Erebus*, Lieutenant Edward Couch, made his will. In the event of his death, his estate was to go to his father, Captain James Couch.

No one knows when or precisely where the unfortunate Edward Couch died. Somewhere in the Canadian Arctic he drew his last breath. But back home in England, four and a half years after he bid his son farewell, James Couch passed away in January 1850.

In 1854 the executor of Edward Couch's estate, a Mr. Ommaney, obtained probate of his will. The esoteric question the Court had to decide was this: Had the father, James Couch, survived his son? Or had the son, Edward Couch, predeceased the father somewhere in the vastness of the Canadian Arctic? The Court had to decide a question of survivorship: Who had died first?

Strangely enough, information provided indirectly by Canadian Inuit was crucial in the Court's difficult decision.

An affidavit of an Arctic explorer was presented as the sole evidence. Dr. John Rae had been involved in the search for Franklin, and provided the following statement:

> I arrived at Repulse Bay, in the Arctic Regions, in the month of August, 1853, and while engaged on such last-mentioned expedition, I, in the Spring and Summer of the year 1854, met with a party of the Esquimaux Tribe, who had in their possession and from whom I purchased and brought with me to this country, on my return thereto in the month of October, 1854, various articles which have . . . been identified . . . as belonging to or as having belonged to the said Sir John Franklin and some of the officers under him.

Rae's affidavit went on to explain that he had obtained information from the Inuit he met in 1854 that in the spring of 1850, another party of Inuit hunting near King William Island had encountered a party of about forty white men travelling southward over the ice, dragging a boat and sledges with them. The white men could not speak Inuktitut, but through signs had communicated to the Inuit that their ships had been crushed by ice. The men, who could only be from Sir John Franklin's expedition, were thin and short of provisions, and obtained some seal meat from the

In Those Days

Inuit. Later that spring, the same group of Inuit discovered on the mainland of North America the bodies of about thirty white men and some graves, and five more dead bodies on a nearby island. Rae's affidavit stated that "some at least of such white men must have survived until the arrival of wild fowl at the said places where such dead bodies were found, as the reports of the firing off of guns were heard by such party of other Esquimaux people, and the fresh bones and feathers of wild geese were noticed by them to be there."

Rae knew from his experience that wild geese would not reach the region until late May or early June. He continued: ". . . so that the fresh bones and feathers of such geese, mentioned, by the said Esquimauxs, as having been seen where such dead bodies were said to have been found . . . lead me to conclude, that some of the white men survived until at least the latter end of the month of May or the beginning of the month of June, in the year 1850."

So some of the white men of Franklin's doomed party had survived until late spring of 1850. The question was: Was Edward Couch among those survivors?

On the answer to that question hung the fate of the estate of Edward Couch. The Court was faced with the impossible question of determining whether Edward Couch was among the white men who had survived in the Arctic until the late spring of 1850, in which case Edward Couch would have survived his father.

Why did it matter?

If Edward was deemed to have died first, his estate would pass to his father, whose estate (now including the value of his son's estate) would pass to his other heirs.

But if Edward was deemed to have survived his father, the father's estate would pass to his designated beneficiaries, which included Edward, and Edward's estate would pass, through common law, to his next of kin. Those next of kin—who included a man named William Couch—may not have been the same as the individuals who would have inherited James's (the father's) estate. So money was at stake.

Lawyers for William Couch, described only as "one of the next of kin of Edward at his death," argued that under British law Edward could not be presumed dead until seven years had passed since he had last been known to have been alive, and since his father had died less than five years after Edward was last known to be alive, the Court must conclude that Edward survived his father, in which case William would stand to inherit some money. Thomas Stilwell, executor of the father's, James Couch's, estate, argued the opposite position.

The case went to Chancery Court for argument. This was a division of the Court that decided points of law on the basis of fairness, rather than a mere application of the law.

The Master of the Rolls, the third most senior judge of England and Wales, was Sir John Romilly, and he had to make the difficult decision. Of course, he had no way of knowing when Edward Couch had died, any more than any of the others involved in the matter. It came down to a question of probability:

> This case involves a question of as great difficulty as any I have ever had to deal with; not only from the want of evidence, but from the tendency of the evidence which exists to create doubt.
>
> The sole question is, whether the son or the father died first. The father died in January, 1850, and the son, who was an active, strong young man, went as mate with Sir John

In Those Days

Franklin in 1845, and the question is whether he died before January, 1850. That is the sole question.

The ordinary presumption that a person who has not been heard of for seven years would apply, if there were nothing else on the subject.

But there was something else on the subject. And that was Inuit evidence, collected by John Rae. The Master, however, in continuing his judgment, ignored the Inuit and incorrectly attributed everything to Rae:

The evidence which exists is that of Dr. Rae. He discovered the remains of various persons who had perished from hunger belonging to the expedition of Sir John Franklin. It is clear that the persons who were seen in April survived the father; they were about forty in number, while the original number was 133, and no identity is proved.

In this state of things, I confess I cannot come to a satisfactory conclusion on the subject. My Chief Clerk is of opinion that the son survived the father, and has made or was about to make a certificate accordingly. He relied on the youth and strength of the son. I cannot see that this conclusion is erroneous. I cannot but express my extreme inability to come to a satisfactory conclusion, but relying on the chances in favour of the youth and strength of the son, I see no reason to differ from the conclusion of the Chief Clerk.

So William Couch benefited from the estate of his unfortunate relative, Edward. He owed his good fortune to Inuit oral evidence provided second-hand to a persistent Arctic explorer.

Murder at Repulse Bay

In 1864 an American explorer from Cincinnati, Charles Francis Hall, launched his second shoestring expedition to the Canadian Arctic in search of survivors of the Franklin expedition, missing since 1845. He was accompanied by his Inuit friends and interpreters, Tookoolito and Ebierbing (properly Ipiirvik), known to whalers as Hannah and Joe, who had spent two winters in the United States with him. Hall had previously explored Frobisher Bay, where he met the well-travelled Inuit couple—they had spent two years in England as teenagers.

Lacking funds for his own ship, he hitched a ride north with whalers, travelling with Captain E. A. Chapel on the *Monticello*. Although he hoped to make his base at Repulse Bay, he and his party were landed at Roe's Welcome Sound, over sixty kilometres south of Wager Bay. He spent his first winter there, before finally moving north to Repulse Bay.

In the fall of 1867 he arranged a contract with the whalers to borrow some men from their crews. Patrick Coleman was one of those men.

The following March, Hall travelled north to the Ooglit Islands, south of Igloolik, in pursuit of more information about alleged sightings of Franklin's men some years previous. From there he explored part of the Melville Peninsula before returning to Repulse Bay. He intended to pass a quiet summer there with the Inuit and his five whalers. But something terrible happened to mar the tranquility he sought.

We will never know with certainty exactly what happened. Hall's journal has a gap of three weeks. But a version of the events appears in the *Narrative of the Second Arctic Expedition Made by Charles F. Hall*, not published until after Hall's own death three years later. The story appears to be in Hall's own words. Perhaps his posthumous editor had found the missing journal pages.

On July 31, according to the narrative, Hall convinced himself that Patrick Coleman and a few other whalers had not been carrying out his orders entirely to his satisfaction. Hall was a volatile man, obsessed with his "mission" to find the fate of Franklin. He had a hair-trigger temper and was often on the verge of violence. He confronted the men at their tent:

> I told them . . . that it became them to be as expeditious as possible whenever I had work for them to do. . . . This was followed by a burst of real mutinous conduct on the part of Pat and Antoine, to which demonstration Sam and Peter seemed to be a party. Pat was the leader, and I felt for my own safety that something must be done to meet so terrible a blow as seemed ready to fall. I appealed to Pat especially to stop his mutinous talk and conduct. I was alone, though

a small distance off were all the Innuits of the tent-village looking upon the scene. Pat was standing in the door of the tent . . . where he was delivering himself of the most rebellious language possible. I made an approach to him, putting my hand up before him, motioning for him to stop. He at once squared himself, doubling up his fists and drawing back in position, as it were, to jump upon and fight me.

Hall considered simply giving Coleman "a good drubbing," but realized that Coleman was a powerful man and that he risked having Coleman's friends come to the man's assistance. Instead, the report continues:

"I demanded of Peter my rifle, which he gave me. I hastened to my tent, laid down the rifle, and seized my Baylie revolver, and went back and faced the leader of the mutinous crowd, and demanded of Pat to know if he would desist in his mutinous conduct. His reply being still more threatening, I pulled the trigger, and he staggered and fell."

After handing the gun over to one of the astonished Inuit, Hall then ran back and assisted Coleman to his tent. "I supposed he could not live five minutes," he wrote, "but a Mightier hand than mine had stayed the ball from a vital part."

Patrick Coleman took two weeks to die. J. E. Nourse, who edited the published account, said that "every effort was made by Hall to save his life by the use of all remedies at his command and by the most careful nursing."

Only two days after Coleman's death, two whaling ships, the *Ansel Gibbs* and the *Concordia*, arrived at Repulse Bay. The remaining four whalers deserted, but Hall chose to remain among the Inuit for one more year.

In Those Days

When he finally returned to the United States, he had some explaining to do. He turned to his patron, Henry Grinnell, for help. The first question that Grinnell needed to have answered was who would have jurisdiction in the case. First he took the matter up before the British government's representatives in Washington. He was surprised at the answer he received. They replied that the shooting had taken place beyond the borders of Canada, so neither the British nor Canadian authorities would have anything to do with it. The American authorities ignored the matter completely.

Hall had killed Patrick Coleman in a legal no-man's land and had gotten off scot-free. Was it murder? Or was it justifiable homicide? The answer to that question turns on whether the killing was justified. It probably wasn't. As Chauncey Loomis pointed out in his excellent biography of Hall, *Weird and Tragic Shores*, there was "no evidence that a mutiny had been planned; whatever Coleman did was on the spur of the moment."

Frank Lailer, the one whaler whom Hall trusted entirely, had not been present at the time of the shooting. Fifty-five years later, he was interviewed by a reporter, and told him that all the sailors were young and that Hall could have controlled them without using a gun. If he had been present, he said, he "could have fixed the matter up."

Had Hall been charged with the murder—it seems appropriate now, under the circumstances, to call it a murder—he could not have pleaded self-defence. He had taken away a rifle from one sailor, and Patrick Coleman was unarmed. It was very fortunate for Hall that the killing took place in a jurisdictional no man's land. He had gotten away with murder.

Years later, another of the whalers, Peter Bayne, gave another possible reason for the shooting. While Hall had been away in the Igloolik area, Bayne and Coleman had had long conversations with the Inuit about the long-lost Franklin expedition. And they learned something new from a native of the Boothia Peninsula. That man told the whalers that one man who had died aboard the ships was buried on shore with great ceremony and that his grave had been covered with something that had turned to stone. Bayne and Coleman understood this to be a cement vault and concluded that such a ceremony would befit only the leader, Franklin himself.

Hall's fanatical interest in Franklin had rubbed off on the whalers. The young men were interested in the subject. The Boothia natives were leaving shortly and so the whalers had them recount the story to the local Inuit so that they, as well as the whalers, would be able to repeat it to Hall on his return. Peter Bayne told his version of the story later to George Jamme, who wrote this:

> The idea in the minds of Bayne and Spearman [another of the whalers], in getting the Boothia natives to recount their story to the local natives, was to have the information for Hall on his return from Fury and Hecla [Strait], and in such shape that it would be useful to him. . . . The motive in doing it was only loyalty on the part of the men. But, to their astonishment, when Hall returned late in June, he rather resented their acts, upbraiding them for their presumption. This is where Hall made a grievous mistake. His attitude was offensive to the men, and they began to lose interest; which latter, in turn, brought about friction. The whole culminated in the shooting of Coleman by Hall, July 31.

In Those Days

The young whalers, in their desire to help Hall unravel the Franklin mystery, had crossed an unseen line that existed only in Hall's tortured mind. They had ventured into unknown territory, impinged on Hall's sacred calling, and invaded what he believed was his mission alone.

Bayne went on to say that Coleman was wrong in his actions and his attitude, "but that the situation had not yet reached the point where it became necessary for Hall to resort to firearms. Hall, however, had to maintain his own standing of respect by the natives."

The crack of a gun and the sight of young Patrick Coleman crumbling to the ground apparently snapped Hall out of his violent reverie. Bayne tells us that "Hall was heartbroken at the happening and tended Coleman as only one such would."

But it was too late for young Patrick Coleman. He lay dead in a tent on the shores of Repulse Bay, the victim of murder.

How Do You Spell Murder?

The Death of Charles Francis Hall

C harles Francis Hall began his third expedition to the Arctic on June 29, 1871. This was the most ambitious one of all. The previous two were in search of information on the missing Franklin expedition, but this one would be an audacious attempt to reach the North Pole by ship. The steamer *Periwinkle* had been completely refitted and had even acquired a new name, more fitted to polar voyaging—the *Polaris*.

Hall's old friend, Captain Sidney O. Budington, was in command of the ship, while Hall would be in charge of the expedition. Or so he thought.

Naively, Hall had said, "I have chosen my own men; men who

will stand by me through thick and thin. Though we may be sur-
rounded by innumerable icebergs, and though our vessel may be
crushed like an eggshell, I believe they will stand by me to the last."

But within a week of leaving the Brooklyn Navy Yard, two
members of the expedition were challenging Hall's authority and
refusing to obey orders. These were Dr. Emil Bessels, a German
physician and naturalist who was the expedition's chief scientist,
and Frederick Meyer, also German, who served as meteorologist.

The ship's company was partly American and partly German,
and the two groups did not get along. There were also two Inuit
families aboard the ship.

The *Polaris* travelled north through Davis Strait, Baffin Bay, and
into Smith Sound. It travelled farther north than any ship had ever
been before. Hall wanted to reach the northern tip of Ellesmere
Island, from which, he hoped, the North Pole would be reached by
sled journeys. But ice stopped the ship at 82°11′ north. The strong
current from the north pushed the ship back into Hall Basin, and it
found refuge in a small cove on the Greenland coast on September
10. Hall named the spot Thank God Harbor. Exactly one month
later, Hall set off with a trusted American companion and Joe and
Hans, the two adult male Inuit, on a reconnaissance trip by sled to
learn about the geography of the area, as preparation for the
hoped-for North Pole sled trip the following spring. They returned, cold but invigorated and optimistic, after a two-week
absence.

Back aboard ship, Hall requested a cup of coffee. He drank the
hot brew, but almost immediately he threw up, complaining of
nausea. He told Joe's wife, Hannah, whom he had known and
trusted for over a decade, that the coffee tasted strange; it had an
uncharacteristic sweet taste, and he felt a burning sensation in his

stomach. But other men had drunk of the same coffee—if indeed it was the same—without suffering any ill effects. Hall, though, had had stomach problems before. For whatever reason, he was the only one to get sick.

Hall asked Dr. Bessels to attend to him. He wanted something to purge his system, but Bessels refused, claiming that Hall was too weak from vomiting already. By the next morning, Hall had a high fever. Bessels injected him with quinine. But Hall's situation deteriorated. He became delirious and openly suggested that he had been poisoned. He suspected the doctor—the two had not gotten along since the beginning of the expedition.

Hall trusted Hannah, and refused to eat any food unless it was prepared by her. By early November he was feeling better. His appetite had returned and the stomach pains were gone. But Bessels wanted to continue treating him, and prevailed upon the ship's chaplain to convince Hall to agree to the treatment. On November 4 Bessels began injecting a substance into Hall's legs. Hall continued to improve. Two days later he took a walk on deck and announced that he was as well as he had ever been.

But the improvement didn't last long. Within another two days he had suffered a relapse. Just past midnight on November 7, a seaman woke Budington to tell him that Hall was dying. Budington, with whom Hall had also had a testy relationship, rushed to his side. Hall was sitting on the edge of his bed. He asked Budington, "How do you spell murder?" Then he stared accusingly at Bessels and said, "Doctor, I know everything that's going on; you can't fool me." Hall was comatose most of the next day. Bessels attended to him in the evening. It was then that Hall spoke his last words. They were to the doctor, and they were quite different from his earlier accusation. He said, "Doctor, you have been very kind to me, and I am obliged to you." Was this a genuine expression of thanks, or were these words spoken with a tone of bitter and resigned irony? Hall never woke up from his sleep, and died in the wee small hours of the morning of November 8, shortly after two in the morning.

Hall was the only person to die on the *Polaris* expedition. Eventually, when the survivors had returned to the United States, a government inquiry was held. George Tyson, the ice-master, spoke of Hall's conviction that someone had poisoned him. He suggested that Captain Sidney O. Budington or the scientist Emil Bessels was responsible. At a subsequent inquiry, a crew member testified that Budington had said "there's a stone off my heart" after Hall's death.

Noah Hayes, a seaman on the expedition, gave damning testimony about Bessels's comments after Hall's death:

"One day I was over at the observatory with Dr. Bessels. I was there a good part of the time about that time in the winter. He appeared to be very light-hearted, and said that Captain Hall's death was the best thing that could happen for the expedition. . . . The next day he was laughing when he mentioned it. I was much hurt at the time and told him I wished he would select someone else as an auditor if he had such a thing to say."

When George Tyson was asked if Hall had accused anyone of trying to poison him, he replied, "Yes, sir, almost everybody; and when I was absent he might accuse me for aught I know. He accused Captain Budington and the doctor of trying to do him an injury."

Bessels told the inquiry about the symptoms that Hall had exhibited and the treatment he had administered. He claimed that Hall had suffered from a stroke and that he was paralyzed on one side. Another shipmate, Meyer, confirmed this, although others who had been present denied it. Government medical experts who examined Bessels's testimony agreed with his diagnosis and his treatment. A stroke would explain some of the symptoms—the alleged paralysis, the slurred speech, the erratic behaviour, and the temporary coma—though it would not explain the high fever.

In the 1960s an Arctic scholar, Chauncey Loomis, was busy preparing a biography of Hall. The hastily reached conclusion that Hall had died of a stroke troubled him. In his book he wrote, "My conclusion was, not that Hall had been murdered, not even that he probably had been murdered, but only that murder was at least possible and plausible." Loomis wanted to know more, and he proposed an audacious plan to investigate Hall's death, almost a century after it had taken place. He wanted an autopsy performed on Hall's body, which he suspected had been well preserved in the frozen ground of Thank God Harbor.

In August of 1968 the famous Arctic pilot Weldy Phipps, flying a Single Otter from Resolute, took Loomis, a pathologist, and two assistants to the gravesite. They dug into the permafrost and exposed Hall's body, draped in the American flag that he had hoped to plant at the North Pole. The body was left in the coffin and the coffin in the ground. The pathologist performed his three-hour autopsy in the agonizing posture necessitated by bending over the grave.

Loomis recounts:

"There was still flesh, a beard, hair on the head, but the eye sockets were empty, the nose was almost gone, and the mouth was pulled into a smile that a few years hence will become the grin of a death's head. The skin, tanned by time and stained by the flag, was tightening on the skull. He was in a strangely beautiful phase in the process of dust returning to dust."

In Those Days

Hall's intestines and stomach had dissolved, as had the brain, which they had hoped to study for signs of the alleged stroke. But the pathologist collected hair and fingernail samples, which continue to grow for some time after death. These were taken to the Centre for Forensic Medicine in Toronto for study.

The results showed that Hall had died of arsenic poisoning, from poison that he had received in the last two weeks of his life. There had likely been no stroke—and indeed, everyone except Bessels and Meyer had denied that there was any paralysis. His symptoms were consistent with arsenic poisoning: the sweet taste, "stomach pains, vomiting, dehydration, intense thirst, feeble pulse, vertigo, stupor, and even mania."

Forensic medicine had determined what had killed Charles Francis Hall: it was an overdose of arsenic.

But who had poisoned him? Several men might have wanted him dead, but Dr. Bessels had unrestricted access to him. He could have administered arsenic with the quinine injections, or put it in the coffee. But Hall also had his own medicine chest. Had he been treating himself in addition to the medicines provided by Bessels, and accidentally poisoned himself? Or did another of the crew kill him?

Chauncey Loomis considered the situation:

"If Hall was murdered, Emil Bessels is the prime suspect. . . . Bessels had the opportunity, the skill, and probably the material, but why would he do it? He had no apparent rational motive."

And so Loomis considered irrational motives. He noted that Bessels was a very difficult man who "scorned Hall, as he apparently scorned many men. Hall was an uneducated boor, but he, Emil Bessels of Heidelberg and Jena, had to serve under him and take his orders. Their relations had been strained at the outset, and

Bessels faced another year, probably another two years, on that tiny ship, suffering the humiliation of an arrogant man in a subservient position."

But Loomis was only able to conclude:

"Perhaps Bessels murdered Hall. Perhaps. The only certain truth that can be found in this case is a knowledge of the inevitable and final elusiveness of the past."

The Execution
of Private Henry

A dolphus Washington Greely, a lieutenant in the US Army, led the Lady Franklin Bay Expedition into the High Arctic in 1881, establishing his base of operations at Fort Conger. The expedition, scientific in nature, was part of the United States' contribution to the first International Polar Year.

In 1883, after two years without a supply ship, Greely and his men abandoned their base and began their desperate retreat south along the Ellesmere Island coast in small boats. Some boats were lost, and with them more of their ever-diminishing food supplies. Able to proceed no farther, Greely established a winter camp at Cape Sabine, a location poor in game.

Over the winter, food—what little remained—was carefully rationed. By springtime everyone was starving. Everyone except, apparently, Private Charles B. Henry. He was the biggest man, and had always been the heaviest eater of the party. Earlier, at Fort Conger, he had put on twenty-five pounds, and had startled some of his campmates by eating raw seal intestines with evident pleasure. Greely and his confidants began to suspect that Private Henry was stealing food. The situation came to a head when half a pound of bacon went missing from a boat where it had been stored. That evening Henry complained of nausea and suddenly vomited into a pan. Another expedition member, Sergeant Frederick, examined the mess and declared it to be half-chewed raw bacon. The other men were incensed—Henry had been proven to be a thief. A trial of sorts ensued, and Henry was put under close arrest and not allowed to leave the hut unaccompanied.

In fact, Private Henry was more than a thief; he was an imposter. His real name was Charles Henry Buck. Although born in Germany, he had an excellent command of English. Described as "splendid soldier material," he had joined the 7th Cavalry in 1876, but was given a dishonourable discharge and a year of hard labour for passing forged cheques. After his release, he had killed a Chinese man in a barroom brawl, then reinvented himself by inverting his name to Charles B. Henry and joining the 5th Cavalry, Greely's old outfit. He had then volunteered to serve under Greely in the Arctic.

By late spring ten men were dead of starvation, and two more were on the point of death. The survivors' meagre rations were supplemented by the tiny shrimp that live in Arctic waters, seaweed, the occasional bird or fox, and leather from thongs, ropes, and articles of clothing. The fragility of life was perhaps summed up in a part of Greely's diary entry for June 4: "To sleep was perchance to die . . ."

And then Private Henry stole again. Greely's summation of this revelation in his journal is almost matter-of-fact: "Henry acknowl-

In Those Days

edged again to me that he had been stealing, and I had a long conversation with him, in which I told him that as he had no conscience he might at least have a little common-sense; that it was evident that if any of the party survived, it must be through unity and fair dealing, otherwise everybody would perish. He promised to deal fairly in the future, and seemed impressed with my caution that he would come to grief if he did not." Doubting Henry's sincerity, Greely gave three of his men an order to shoot Henry immediately if he were seen eating any food not issued to him or "appropriating any article of provisions."

The following day was June 6. Sergeant Frederick caught Henry stealing shrimp from the messpot. Later in the day, Greely questioned Henry on the latter's return from the old winter quarters, and Henry admitted taking sealskin thongs from the stores there, contrary to orders. Greely noted that he was "bold in his admissions, and showed neither fear nor contrition."

Greely immediately wrote out an order for Henry's execution. Addressed to Sergeants Brainard, Long, and Frederick, it read: "Notwithstanding promises given by Private C. B. Henry yesterday, he has since acknowledged to me having tampered with seal thongs, if not other food, at the old camp. This pertinacity and audacity is the destruction of this party if not at once ended. Private Henry will be shot to-day, all care being taken to prevent his injuring any one, as his physical strength is greater than that of any two men. Decide the manner of death by two ball and one blank cartridge. This order is imperative, and absolutely necessary for any chance of life."

Private Henry was shot at two in the afternoon on that "fine, warm, clear day" on the shores of Ellesmere Island. A search of his effects revealed many hidden items of sealskin—items that could have been eaten in desperation, and should have been shared with others. The survivors agreed that Henry's fate was merited.

After rescue, Greely duly reported the execution to his superiors, and asked for a court of inquiry. The secretary of war, however, concluded that Greely's order was justified, and declined to take any action.

The Killing
of Ross Marvin

On March 1, 1909, a determined band of American explorers and Inughuit from northwestern Greenland left Cape Columbia, at the northern tip of Ellesmere Island, bound for the North Pole. Their leader was Robert Peary, whose expeditions to northern Greenland had spanned a period of eighteen years. This would be his final attempt to claim the ultimate geographical prize for which he had yearned so long.

Peary's method involved advance parties preceding him on the route northward to lay out caches of supplies for his own group and their dogs. Other parties, also carrying supplies for later stages of Peary's dash for the pole, would accompany him to perform specific tasks along the route—one was a pickaxe brigade to clear the route ahead for Peary. At various points, Peary would take over the other party's supplies and a sledge party would be sent back to

Cape Columbia with only enough provisions for their own lightly laden return.

One of these support parties was led by Ross Marvin, a young graduate of Cornell University. He had left the United States with Peary in the summer of the previous year and wintered in the High Arctic, revelling in the outdoor life and in the opportunity to prove himself against new and unique challenges. At Cape Columbia, Peary placed him in charge of a group of three Inughuit: Qilluttooq, his younger cousin Inukitsupaluk, and Aarqioq. The trip north to supply Peary was rough on Marvin. He suffered from frostbite to his heels and toes. Bob Bartlett, the leader of another party, said, "All the skin was taken off both heels and all his toes. He was in a sorry plight, but as far as I could see, it did not worry him in the least." Marvin and his men accompanied Peary to 86°38′ north before the commander ordered their return to Cape Columbia on March 26.

When the three Inughuit reached the *Roosevelt*, Peary's ship frozen in on the Ellesmere coast, it was without Ross Marvin and with the tragic tale of an accident. On their return on April 10, Ross Marvin had fallen through a lead, and had drowned. They had been unable to recover his body.

Peary had continued north after the two parties separated, and claimed to have reached the North Pole on April 6 (a claim widely disputed ever since). He returned to Cape Columbia on April 23, where he learned the sad news of Marvin's death. In September, on Peary's return to America, it was to glory, and ultimately to controversy. Hidden within the press's adulation of Peary were brief reports of the accidental drowning of Ross Marvin. But he was quickly forgotten.

Amazingly, a different story—the truth—came out over a decade

later. Qilluttooq had been converted to Christianity by the missionary at Thule in December 1923, and had had a confession to make
to clear his conscience. Ross Marvin had not drowned on that dis-
tant day as the party sledged southward from their farthest north.
Rather, Qilluttooq had shot him.

The circumstances, he recounted, were these: Marvin's behaviour
had become irrational. He was extremely demanding. He forced
the Inughuit to cross dangerous stretches of new ice over barely
frozen leads instead of waiting for more solid ice, as the Inughuit
suggested. He accused the Inughuit of laziness. Twice Marvin himself fell through the ice and the Inughuit rescued him. Then Inukitsupaluk, the youngest member of the group, fell ill. Marvin ordered
the others to abandon him. As Marvin began to load Inukitsupaluk's
sled, Qilluttooq asked the younger man to pass him his rifle and
calmly shot Marvin through the head. They sank his body through
a hole in the ice and waited two days for Inukitsupaluk to regain
his strength. During this time they devised the story that they
would tell on their return to the *Roosevelt*.

In 1925 Knud Rasmussen, the Danish-Greenlandic ethnographer
and explorer, heard about Qilluttooq's confession, and questioned
the Inughuit about the matter. Inukitsupaluk told him: "I saw
Qilluttooq on a big piece of rough ice and he yelled to me that I
should bring him his rifle. He had seen a seal in the open water. I
brought his rifle and went back to the sled. I heard a shot a moment
after and expected that Qilluttooq had shot the seal. But right away
he came over to me and told me what had happened. He had shot
Marvin in order to save my life."

Knud Rasmussen reported his findings to the Danish government:

In no single instance is there any reason to doubt that the reports of the Eskimos are truthful. An entire winter's fatiguing travel got the best of Marvin's nerves, and in a fit of anger he acted without thinking . . . the Eskimos looked upon his action [in threatening to leave Inukitsupaluk behind] as if he really meant it, and for this reason, I feel, they were fully justified in considering the situation dangerous. . . . As the matter stands now, I don't see how Qilluttooq can in any way be held responsible for the sad outcome of the trouble.

No charges were ever brought.

Christian Klengenberg

An Arctic Enigma

K lengenberg is a family name well known in the central Canadian Arctic. The name is Danish, but is now also an Inuit name, as it has been for some generations. This article will tell about the adventurous young cook from Denmark who brought the name to the central Canadian Arctic. It will tell also about some of the controversies that tarnished his name and followed him through life.

Christian Klengenberg was twenty-four years old when he jumped ship in Point Barrow, Alaska, in 1893 and began his life among the Inuit. Soon he married an Inupiaq woman, whose name he recorded as Gremnia. She was later more commonly known as Qimniq. He supported himself through whaling and trading.

FIGURE 1: Sir Martin Frobisher, leader of the expedition that led to the first documented contact between Inuit and white people.

SOURCE: THE BODLEIAN LIBRARY, UNIVERSITY OF OXFORD, L.P. 50.

FIGURE 2: Henry Hudson and his son. Hudson was captain of the ship *Discovery* until his crew organized a mutiny, casting him, his son John, and seven other men adrift in a shallop.

SOURCE: THE LAST VOYAGE OF HENRY HUDSON, EXHIBITED 1881, THE HON. JOHN COLLIER (1850–1934) © TATE, LONDON 2015.

FIGURE 3: Samuel Hearne. On an expedition from Churchill to the Coppermine River in 1771, Hearne documented the killing of Inuit by his Chipewyan travelling companions at Bloody Fall. SOURCE: GLENBOW ARCHIVES, NA-3548-1.

FIGURE 4: Sir John Franklin, leader of the expedition on which Robert Hood lost his life.
SOURCE: KENN HARPER COLLECTION.

FIGURE 5: Charles Francis Hall, who murdered Patrick Coleman at Repulse Bay. It is likely that Hall himself was murdered in northern Greenland on his next expedition.
SOURCE: KENN HARPER COLLECTION.

TOOKOOLITO, C. F. HALL, AND EBIERBING.

FIGURE 6: Tookoolito (Hannah), Charles Francis Hall, and Ebierbing (Joe). The Inuit couple accompanied Hall on his three Arctic expeditions.

SOURCE: FROM *ARCTIC RESEARCHES AND LIFE AMONG THE ESQUIMAUX*, BY CHARLES FRANCIS HALL. NEW YORK: HARPER & BROS., 1864.

JOE, HANNAH, AND CHILD.

FIGURE 7: Tookoolito (Hannah) and her husband, Ebierbing (Joe), with their adopted daughter, Panik.

SOURCE: FROM *ARCTIC RESEARCHES AND LIFE AMONG THE ESQUIMAUX*, BY CHARLES FRANCIS HALL. NEW YORK: HARPER & BROS., 1864.

FIGURE 8: Dr. Emil Bessels, chief scientist on Charles Francis Hall's *Polaris* expedition.
SOURCE: KENN HARPER COLLECTION.

FIGURE 9: Sidney O. Budington, captain of the *Polaris*.
SOURCE: KENN HARPER COLLECTION.

FIGURE 10: George Tyson, ice-master of the *Polaris*.
SOURCE: KENN HARPER COLLECTION.

CAPTAIN TYSON IN HIS ARCTIC COSTUME.

FIGURE 11: George Tyson in his Arctic costume.
SOURCE: KENN HARPER COLLECTION.

FIGURE 12: A sailor at the grave of Charles Francis Hall in northwestern Greenland.
SOURCE: KENN HARPER COLLECTION.

FIGURE 13: Participants in Adolphus Washington Greely's scientific expedition to the High Arctic in 1881. The expedition ended in disaster when supply ships failed to arrive for two consecutive years. The unfortunate Private Henry is standing sixth from the left.
SOURCE: KENN HARPER COLLECTION.

FIGURE 14: Lieutenant Adolphus Washington Greely.
SOURCE: KENN HARPER COLLECTION.

FIGURE 15: Ross Marvin, a member of Robert Peary's 1909 expedition to the North Pole.

SOURCE: KENN HARPER COLLECTION.

FIGURE 16: Qilluttooq, an Inughuit member of Peary's expedition to the North Pole. Qilluttooq shot Ross Marvin when his behaviour became irrational and dangerous.

SOURCE: PHOTO COURTESY STEPHEN LORING, ARCTIC STUDIES CENTER ARCHIVES, SMITHSONIAN INSTITUTION.

FIGURE 17: American explorer Robert Peary, most famous for claiming to reach the North Pole in 1909. This claim has been disputed ever since.

SOURCE: KENN HARPER COLLECTION.

FIGURE 18: Captain Christian Klengenberg at Baillie Island, July 1916.
SOURCE: LIBRARY AND ARCHIVES CANADA / MIKAN 4105102.

FIGURE 19: The Klengenberg family at Cape Bathurst, ca. 1916.
SOURCE: GLENBOW ARCHIVES, PD-395-1-37.

FIGURE 20: Inspector Francis French in 1917. French made a five-thousand-mile dog-team patrol, known as the Bathurst Inlet Patrol, in search of the murderers of Harry Radford and George Street.

SOURCE: GLENBOW ARCHIVES, NA-40-41.

FIGURE 21: Akulack and his wife in 1915. Akulack accompanied Harry Radford and George Street to Bathurst Inlet in 1911–12. They were murdered there in June 1912.
SOURCE: GLENBOW ARCHIVES, NA-2306-9.

FIGURE 22: Father Jean-Baptiste Rouvière and Father Guillaume LeRoux. Both men were murdered in 1913 on a missionary trip to the Copper Inuit.
SOURCE: KENN HARPER COLLECTION.

He returned north. But his acquittal meant little to many in Alaska. It was widely believed that he was guilty of the murder of Jackson Paul.

Many years later, another incident occurred that reminded old-timers all over again about the suspicions that clouded Klengenberg's reputation.

In 1924 Klengenberg sailed his own ship, the *Maid of New Orleans*, from Alaska into Canadian waters, filled with trade goods for his post on Victoria Island. But first he stopped at Herschel Island, where he was informed of a Canadian government policy that prevented the landing of foreign goods in Canada from American ships. Klengenberg was a naturalized American citizen and his ship was American-registered. The policy therefore applied to him and would prevent him from bartering his trade goods with Inuit for furs. Klengenberg argued for the right to continue on to Victoria Island with the goods, but to land only items sufficient to supply his own immediate family.

Permission was granted, on condition that he stop at the RCMP detachment on Baillie Island. There a young constable, MacDonald, was ordered to accompany Klengenberg to ensure that goods for trade were not landed at Victoria Island.

The trip to Klengenberg's post proceeded without incident. Klengenberg was reunited for a time with his family, then began the return journey to Baillie Island. But on this leg of the voyage, Constable MacDonald mysteriously disappeared. Klengenberg himself recounted the incident succinctly in his memoirs: "He must have fallen overboard, but none of the crew saw the accident happen. . . . Nothing was ever seen of him again."

A search of the icy waters ensued. A crew member took to a rowboat and returned from his search with MacDonald's caribou-skin parka and his notebook—he had found them floating in the water. The mate, Henry Larsen, later in life to become famous in these same waters as the captain of the RCMP vessel *St. Roch*, was not suspicious, writing many years after the fact, "It was impossible to ascertain why or how the constable had fallen overboard. We thought that perhaps he had gone up forward, where there was no railing, and had lost his balance while he was standing there. With the noisy engine going it would have been practically impossible for the helmsman to hear any cries for help, and from where he was standing he could not see the bow." Larsen did find one detail perplexing though, adding, "How the constable had managed to get his parka off and put his notebook on top of it remained a mystery."

A later writer, historian H. G. Jones, took up this question when he wrote, "No one answered another obvious question: Why would, or how could, a man fighting for his life in icy water remove his caribou-skin parka and neatly place his notebook atop it before drowning?"

Both Larsen's and Jones's observations overlook one possibility, however. If MacDonald had just come from his cabin before toppling overboard, it's possible that he wasn't even wearing his caribou-skin parka. He may have been carrying it, intending to put it on while on deck, and fallen overboard while holding it. Removing the notebook from a pocket (if he wasn't carrying that, too) might have been the last responsible act of a dedicated officer.

The ship reached Baillie Island with the flag at half-mast, and Klengenberg hastened to the post to report the drowning of Constable MacDonald to the police officers there. Then he continued on to Herschel Island to face Inspector Caulkin. Many on the island remembered the acquittal of seventeen years earlier, and doubted Klengenberg's story. Some thought that he had landed more stores at Victoria Island than the inspector had authorized, hoping to profit from their sale, and that MacDonald knew about it and would have reported it to his superiors. This, they surmised, might have served as motive for disposing of MacDonald. Inspector Caulkin conducted a thorough investigation. He had everything taken from the ship to the police storehouse. Henry Larsen later wrote, "Every single item was checked off on the list the captain had for customs purposes, and luckily for him, every item missing was found in MacDonald's notebook, which we had fished out of the water. This proved that everything was in order."

The case had aroused a great deal of interest because the unfortunate constable who had drowned happened to be the grandson of Canada's first prime minister, Sir John A. MacDonald. But with Caulkin's investigation having shown that no trade items were illegally landed at Victoria Island, no charges were warranted. The event was deemed to be a tragic accident. Once again, Christian Klengenberg had been vindicated.

Klengenberg had spent the years between his 1907 acquittal and the 1924 accident living in the western and central Canadian Arctic with his Inuit family, often travelling back to Herschel Island and Alaska.

He was the first white man to trade with the little-known Inuit of Victoria Island. Communication with them was difficult and he often used his daughter, Weena, who spoke Inupiaq, as an interpreter. Klengenberg had found what he had earlier dreamed about. "I had found a land and a people where I could be the first to trade," he wrote, "and I made up my mind that eventually I would have my own ship and my own goods and go back with my family to Victoria Island and found a permanent trading post."

In fact, Klengenberg established several trading posts. These included one that he built in 1916 at Cape Kendall, on the mainland near the mouth of the Coppermine River. Three years later he built a permanent post at Rymer Point on Victoria Island. His Inupiaq wife, Qimniq, has been described as "shrewd and energetic." She was a tremendous asset to a white trader in a new territory, where she was able to communicate with the native Inuit in their own language.

The enterprising Dane was for many years able to evade much of the red tape of customs regulations that accompanied the insidious creep of southern bureaucracy into the Arctic and made real the once imaginary line that separated Canada from Alaska just west of Herschel Island. Eventually officialdom caught up with him in 1924, the year of Constable MacDonald's drowning. The following year, Klengenberg gave up his American citizenship—he had become naturalized many years earlier—and became a Canadian. He hoped that the Canadian government might recognize in some way his contribution to Canadian sovereignty in the Far North. He told a biographer in 1931, "I would like a definite grant of land to myself and my heirs on Victoria Island. . . . Because my proper and continuous occupation helped to confirm Canadian title to what may provide valuable stations for the new air routes across the top of the world." His hope was in vain. No land was ever granted.

Christian Klengenberg and Qimniq had a large family. His oldest daughter, Weena, married a Dane, Storker Storkersen. Etna married an Inupiaq man from Point Barrow, Ikey Bolt, and they eventually took over the Rymer Point post. Lena married George Avakana, and they ran a trading post at Cape Krusenstern. The oldest son, Patsy, joined the Canadian Arctic Expedition at only fifteen years of age as an assistant to the anthropologist Diamond Jenness. Two years later he acted as translator for a murder trial in Edmonton. Other children in the Klengenberg clan were Andrew, Jorgen, Bob, and Diamond.

Qimniq and her older daughters were responsible for introducing Alaskan fashions to the Canadian Inuit with whom they lived, particularly the style of parka known as the Mother Hubbard, so different from the parkas used in the eastern Arctic. The Mother Hubbard, still popular today, is a lasting legacy of the Klengenbergs.

Many descendants of Christian and Qimniq Klengenberg live today in the communities of the central and western Arctic, especially Qurluqtuuq (Coppermine) and Uluksaqtuuq (Holman). They include community leaders, artists, sculptors, and craftsmen.

Klengenberg was a larger-than-life character, the stuff of which legends are made. Vilhjalmur Stefansson wrote of him that he "had a reputation for enterprise, energy, and fearlessness—but he was also known to be unscrupulous, ruthless and two-faced. . . . I came to accept Klinkenberg [sic] as a kind of legend in which I only half believed." But this is a case of the pot calling the kettle black, for the pejoratives that Stefansson applied to Klengenberg apply equally well to Stefansson himself, an incompetent expedition leader and purveyor of falsehoods, responsible for the deaths of many men under his charge.

Christian Klengenberg died in Vancouver in 1931 while visiting his daughter. His son, Patsy, carried his ashes home to Victoria Island.

Whether Klengenberg murdered Jackson Paul in 1906 will probably never be known. But it's obvious that he was not culpable in the death of Constable MacDonald in 1924, despite the aspersions cast upon him. He was a tough man raising a large biracial family

In Those Days

at the edge of the known world in one of the harshest environments known to mankind. He ignored the law when it suited him, and followed it when he had no choice. He was an explorer, a trader, and the founder of an Arctic dynasty. He also had a sense of humour—among the many ships and barges that he owned at various times was a scow named the *Homely Hippopotamus*.

Can a Man Be Mistaken for a Seal?

T he covering report from the Churchill police detachment to the Officer Commanding the Royal North-West Mounted Police was brief. Superintendent Moodie was forwarding to headquarters the report of an unfortunate killing that had happened at Fullerton detachment, near Repulse Bay, late in the spring of 1909.

Attached to his report was that of a young constable, Charles R. MacMillan, stationed at Fullerton. His report began with the terse statement that he had to report "the following painful occurrence." He then wrote that on the evening of June 22, he and two other constables were looking out over the sea ice with a telescope and saw a large seal on the ice, apparently about two miles offshore. MacMillan decided that he would like to get a shot at it.

In Those Days

"I walked to within 600 yards or so of the object, and then lay down on the ice to crawl nearer without alarming the animal," he wrote. "I crawled towards it for about 200 yards or more, and then was stopped by a large pool of water. I was afraid to stand up and wade through it, for fear of alarming the seal, and did not like to risk a shot at the distance, as from my position face down close to the ice, the object did not show up very well." He reported that during all this time the seal had moved a little but had not changed its position either backward or forward.

Finally the young constable took a shot, and the object disappeared. MacMillan then described his horror at what he saw when he ran towards the "seal" he had shot: "On standing up I saw it, and immediately ran towards it. I ran for some yards when I suddenly stopped, horrified, and I saw it was a man lying face up. I compelled myself to go up to him, and found he was dead. He was an Iwillik [an Inuit from the Aivilik group] called Charlie."

MacMillan had shot Charlie with one clean shot through the neck.

Earlier that afternoon, Constable Walker and Corporal Joyce had taken a walk on the ice to the floe edge. On their return they had passed quite close to a large seal on the ice. Back at the police barracks they had scanned the sea ice with a telescope and thought they saw the same seal in roughly the same place. This was the seal that MacMillan had set off in search of.

After his fatal shot, MacMillan raced back to the post and reported to Joyce, his superior, what he had done. Joyce, accompanied by Constable MacDiarmid and an Inuit assistant named Joe, went immediately to examine the fresh corpse lying on the ice. Joyce reported, "The body was lying face up in a low place on the ice, a loaded rifle was on the ice near the body, and a piece of bear's skin, such as is used by natives for crawling seals, was under the hips." Poor Charlie had perhaps been stalking the same large seal that the police had seen earlier.

Another native employed at the Fullerton post, whom the whalers had given the nickname "Bye and Bye," helped Charlie's grieving wife and stepmother to bury the body. Four reports were written. MacMillan himself wrote, "The natives say the man was fast asleep, and that this same kind of accident has happened with them."

Joyce corroborated this, writing that the Inuit said the man had probably fallen fast asleep on the ice.

Superintendent Moodie's brief report concluded, "I may say from my own experience that it is a very easy thing to mistake a native crawling for, or lying in wait for seal for the actual animal itself."

And there the matter was left. No further investigation was made. It was an accidental death, the result of a tragic error by an inexperienced officer.

The Killing of Radford and Street

In 1909 Harry Radford, a wealthy sportsman from New York, went north to collect specimens for the United States Biological Survey and the Smithsonian Institution. "Handsome Harry" was known to veteran northern travellers and the police as insensitive, easy to anger, difficult, and headstrong. Once, in the sub-Arctic, he had threatened to sue a police officer who had refused to allow him to shoot a wood buffalo. Joining him in Fort Smith in the western Canadian sub-Arctic was a strong young surveyor, twenty-two-year-old George Street of Ottawa, a young man with some experience working in the wilderness in Alberta and Saskatchewan.

Radford had an ambitious plan. He and his companion would paddle and portage from Fort Smith all the way to Chesterfield

Inlet on the Hudson Bay coast, then sledge northwest to Bathurst Inlet, continue from there along the coast to Fort McPherson on the Mackenzie Delta, and from there to the Yukon. Much of this country was unexplored. Street was made to sign an unusual contract: he would risk his own life to protect Radford's; if food became short, he would get less than his share; and he could keep no journals.

The two men left Fort Smith on June 27, 1911. Two Yellowknife Dene were hired to help with the load, but they soon deserted, complaining of poor treatment. The two travellers reached the central Keewatin late in the fall, too late to go any farther. They decided to winter at Schulz Lake, and were put up in an addition to the snowhouse of the local headman, Akulack.

Street took immediately to this environment—the cold didn't bother him, the food was agreeable, the people were easygoing. Radford, on the other hand, was impatient and impulsive. He sought guides for the spring trip to Bathurst Inlet. Two Inuit, nicknamed Cockney and Boozer, reluctantly agreed to accompany the white men, but when Boozer backed out on his agreement because Radford refused to leave supplies for his wife, Radford threatened to shoot the man. Boozer called his bluff, telling him to shoot, and Radford backed down. In the end, Akulack agreed to be their guide. The trip to Bathurst Inlet took six weeks, the party arriving there in early May. Radford began exploring and mapping this "last strip remaining unexplored of the continental coast of North America." And then, silence.

The two-man expedition seemingly vanished. Nothing more was heard of them until June 1913, when Akulack arrived at the Hudson's Bay Company trading post to report to the manager there that both Radford and Street had been killed by Inuit at

In Those Days

Bathurst Inlet. The post manager duly reported the alleged crime to the authorities in the south. Canada authorized a special patrol of the Royal Northwest Mounted Police to investigate, and set aside $70,656 to cover its cost.

This was a staggering sum for the time—but more than tracking down a murderer was at stake. This patrol gave the police the opportunity to exert their authority in a vast, unexplored area. On July 31, 1914, a patrol left Halifax for Chesterfield Inlet by schooner. It was under the command of Inspector W. J. Beyts, Sgt. Major Thomas Caulkin, and a few constables. In the Arctic, they continued on to Baker Lake. With that as their base, despite herculean efforts over two years, they failed to reach Bathurst Inlet.

In June 1916 Beyts was relieved of his command and replaced with Inspector Francis French, a nephew of the force's first commissioner. In May of the following year, French, Caulkin, and a number of Inuit dog-drivers and interpreters finally succeeded in reaching Bathurst Inlet. There, raising their hands high above their heads, a traditional greeting of peace, they met the Inuit of that isolated area.

French immediately got down to business. He travelled about Bathurst Inlet, asking the Inuit what they knew about the alleged murders. He wrote out sworn depositions from eleven men and one woman, most of whom had witnessed the killings. Their stories were all the same. About five years earlier, the two white men had arrived at North Quadyuk Island. The older man, the leader, was called Ishumatok (the one who thinks), the younger one Kiuk (wood), because he was so strong. Ishumatok was extremely bad-tempered, so much so that some people thought he was possessed by a spirit. Neither could speak the language of the people, and communication was only by signs.

The guide who had brought them to Bathurst Inlet, Akulack, had departed, so the two explorers needed a new guide. Harla and Kaneak were recruited, but Kaneak changed his mind because his wife had fallen and hurt herself and he wished to stay behind and help her. Radford was incensed at this change of heart and began to talk very loudly. No one knew what he was saying. Suddenly he began to beat Kaneak with a dog whip, hitting him many times on the head and in the face. Street tried to restrain him but couldn't. Radford then dragged Kaneak over to a hole in the ice, and the Inuit thought he was going to force him down the hole. Another man, Okituk, grabbed Radford, while Hulalark stabbed him through the back with a snow knife (a large metal knife made for cutting snow blocks).

Street ran for the sled. No one knew if he was running to get his gun, with which to protect Radford, or if he was running for his life. But the Inuit could not chance that he would come back with a weapon. Okituk chased after him and held him. Another man, Amegealnik, stabbed him in the back. Street died immediately. Radford was still alive, so Hulalark slit his throat to end his life. Their bodies were wrapped in skins and left on the ice.

The Inuit unanimously described Radford as having treated them badly—earlier he had chased one of them with a knife—but thought his young companion to be a good man. Amegealnik, who had killed him, later offered the premium pelts from his take of white fox to the missionary W. H. B. Hoare, to send to Street's family as a way of making amends.

The police concluded that Amegealnik and Hulalark, who were not in Bathurst Inlet at the time of their investigation and therefore not questioned directly by the police, had acted in their own defence. French had been instructed by the government to "ascertain the facts." His orders stated, "It is assumed there was provocation, if so it is not the intention of the Government to proceed with prosecution." Accordingly, French exonerated the two men.

In fact, the police recognized that the Inuit had dealt with Radford and Street according to the principles of Inuit law. The Inuit of the camp had perceived a threat to their individual and collective safety, a threat serious enough that it could not be dealt with by reason alone. For the safety of those residing in the camp, the men of the group had had to take action that unfortunately resulted in the deaths of the strangers.

Inspector French gave the Inuit a warning that his decision in this case would be the last such verdict they would see. If they killed or harmed white men again, he told them, "the culprits would be taken away and never return." This was an ominous threat. As if to confirm it, an aging shaman told the police that he had observed a bad spirit following the police patrol's sleds as they had come into camp.

After a number of false starts, French's patrol returned to Baker Lake on January 29, 1918. The longest, most difficult police patrol in the history of the force was at an end. French himself had travelled 5,153 miles and had rendered an appropriate verdict in the case.

Sinnisiak and Uluksuk

In the summer of 1913 two Oblate missionaries—Father Jean-Baptiste Rouvière, who had served four years among the Dogrib and Hareskin Indians at Fort Good Hope, and Father Guillaume LeRoux, a man described as highly educated, a gentleman and a philosopher, but given to frequent expressions of hot temper—left the Roman Catholic mission at Fort Norman on the Mackenzie River to go northeast to proselytize among the Inuit of the Arctic coast, the people popularized by the explorer Vilhjalmur Stefansson as the Copper Eskimos. The priests were in a hurry; reports had reached Fort Norman that a Church of England missionary was moving into Coronation Gulf, and the Catholics were rushing to forestall him.

Soon, though, reports began to reach Fort Norman that Inuit had been seen wearing priest's cassocks. When the priests were

In Those Days

never heard from again, it was feared they had been murdered. Catholic authorities requested that the Royal North-West Mounted Police investigate. So in June of 1915, Inspector Charles Deering ("Denny") LaNauze, described as a handsome, strapping young man, six feet tall and magnificently built, set out to investigate.

LaNauze was well educated and had a reputation for fairness. He was accompanied by two constables and an Inuit interpreter, Ilavinik, who was made a special constable for the investigation.

In fact, the two priests had been murdered in November of 1913, only a few months after leaving Fort Norman. LaNauze learned of the events from Koeha, an elder of the Copper Inuit. Koeha told the policeman what had happened, using the names the Inuit had given to the two priests: Kuleavik for Rouvière and Ilagoak for LeRoux.

His story went like this: At an Inuit camp, there had been trouble between LeRoux and an Inuk named Kormik, who had stolen a rifle from one of the priests and hidden it. When the priest discovered the theft, angry words were exchanged. Kormik wanted to kill the priest on the spot, and Koeha himself had helped LeRoux escape. But two days after the priests left Kormik's camp, two young men, Uluksuk and Sinnisiak, set out to follow them. Koeha recounted:

> They went to a place near Bloody Falls . . . on the west bank of the Coppermine River. They were all walking along, Sinnisiak took a knife, and stabbed Ilagoak in the back. Kuleavik started to run away and Sinnisiak told Uluksuk, "You finish this man, I will shoot the other." Sinnisiak grabbed the white man's rifle and shot Kuleavik. . . . I asked Uluksuk, "What did you kill the white men for?" and he said, "I did not want to

kill them; Sinnisiak told me to kill them." I asked him if he eat any part of the man, the same as he would do if he killed caribou, and he said, "I eat some of his guts."

Other Inuit recounted their version of the events to LaNauze with considerable hesitation. They were afraid. John Hornby, another white man who had travelled through their land, had once told them that if they killed a white man, more white men would come and kill them all.

In the spring of 1916, LaNauze finally arrested the two suspects without resistance at Coronation Gulf. Sinnisiak voluntarily gave a statement: "Ilagoak was carrying a rifle. He was mad with us when we had started back from their camp, and I could not understand his talk . . . I asked Ilagoak if he was going to kill me, and he nodded his head."

Despite this misunderstanding, they continued to travel together. Sinnisiak continued his story:

We went a little way and Uluksuk and I started to talk and Ilagoak put his hand on my mouth. Ilagoak was very mad and was pushing me. I was thinking hard and crying and very scared . . . I wanted to go back, but I was afraid. I got hot inside my body and every time Ilagoak pulled out the rifle I was very much afraid. . . . I said to Uluksuk, "I think they will kill us; I can't get back now, I was thinking I will not see my people any more, I will try and kill him."

After another altercation between the priest and Sinnisiak, involving more pushing and shoving by the priest, Sinnisiak acted. "Then Ilagoak turned around and saw me," he said, continuing:

75

In Those Days

He looked away from me and I stabbed him in the back with a knife. I then told Uluksuk, "You take the rifle." Ilagoak ran ahead of the sled and Uluksuk went after him . . . Uluksuk and Ilagoak were wrestling for the rifle, and after that Uluksuk finished up Ilagoak.

The other man ran away when he saw Ilagoak die . . . I then said to Uluksuk, "Give me the rifle." He gave it to me. The first time I shot I did not hit him, the second I got him. The priest sat down when the bullet hit him. I went after him with the knife, when I was close to him. . . . The father fell down on his back. Uluksuk struck first with the knife and did not strike him; the second time he got him. The priest lay down and was breathing a little, when I struck him across the face with an axe I was carrying. I cut his legs with the axe. I killed him dead.

Each man ate a piece of LeRoux's liver.

LaNauze listened patiently to Sinnisiak's tale. At Bernard Harbour, he sat as Justice of the Peace and committed Sinnisiak and Uluksuk to stand trial. He escorted them to Herschel Island, from where they were taken to Edmonton.

On August 14, 1917, the trial began. But the Crown had a surprise in store for the defence. They tried only Sinnisiak, and only for the murder of Father Rouvière. It was a trial by a jury of six. Judge Horace Harvey presided. James E. Wallbridge acted as defence counsel. In his opening address, the loquacious Charles Cursolles McCaul, Crown counsel, made it clear that this was no ordinary murder trial, but one intended to extend the reach of Canadian law to the remotest part of the country. "These remote savages," he said, really cannibals, the Eskimo of the Arctic have got to be taught to recognize the authority of the British Crown, and that the authority of the Crown and of the Dominion of Canada, of which these countries are a part, extends to the furthermost limits of the frozen North. It is necessary that they should understand that they are *under the Law,* just in the same way as it was necessary to teach the Indians of the Indian Territories and of the North West Territories that they were under the Law; that they must regulate their lives and dealings with their fellow men, of whatever race, white men or Indians, according to, at least, the main outstanding principles of that law, which is part of the law of civilization, and that this law must be respected on the barren lands of North America, and on the shores of the Arctic Ocean, and on the ice of the Polar Seas, even as far as the Pole itself.

They have got to be taught to respect the principles of Justice—and not merely to submit to it, but to learn that they are entitled themselves to resort to it, to resort to the law, to resort to British justice, and to take advantage of it the same way as anybody else does. The code of the savage, an eye for an eye, a tooth for a tooth, a life for a life must be replaced among them by the code of civilization.

They must learn to know, whether they are Eskimo or not, that death is not the only penalty for a push or a shove, or a swearword, or for mere false dealing; that for these offences our civilization and justice do not allow a man to be shot or to be stabbed, to be killed or murdered. They have got to learn that even if slight violence is used it will not justify murder. . . .

If that is their idea, their notion of justice, I hope when

the result of this trial is brought back to the Arctic regions that all such savage notions will be effectually dispelled. . . .

The great importance of this trial lies in this: that for the first time in history these people . . . will be brought in contact with and will be taught what is white-man's justice.

But then McCaul, perhaps impressed by his own eloquence, spoiled his otherwise brilliant address. When he continued, it became clear that his real purpose was to make the Arctic safe for white men, who would come to explore and exploit the region's resources:

You, gentlemen, can understand how important this is: white men travel through the barren lands; white men live on the shores of Bear Lake; white men go to the shores of the Arctic Ocean; and if we are to believe the reports of the copper deposits near the mouth of the Coppermine River, many white men more may go to investigate and to work the mines. The Eskimo must be made to understand that the lives of others are sacred, and that they are not justified in killing on account of any mere trifle that may ruffle or annoy them.

Sinnisiak, uncomprehending and dressed in skin clothing, as befitted a show trial, fell asleep during McCaul's lengthy address. Bizarrely, a tub of ice water had been placed near him, so that he could dip his feet in whenever he needed to cool off.

The witnesses and the accused were sworn in with an unusual oath. The interpreter, Ilavinik, was at a loss to even understand, let alone translate, the normal oath regarding the truth, the whole truth, and nothing but the truth. A more down-to-earth substitute was allowed: "Whatever you speak now, you speak straight; do not speak with two tongues."

The defence argued for acquittal, on the grounds that the Inuk knew nothing of the white man's law and should not be judged by it, and that he had acted in self-defence, thinking he was about to be killed by the priest. What Sinnisiak had committed, Wallbridge argued, was not murder but justifiable homicide. In his charge to the jury, Chief Justice Harvey argued against Wallbridge's case for acquittal. But the unexpected happened. The jury deliberated for little more than an hour, and came back with a verdict of not guilty. The trial had lasted four days.

The Crown counsel and the judge were outraged. They felt the jury had been influenced by a sympathetic local press and by public sentiment. McCaul even suggested that some jurors held an anti-Catholic bias and were reluctant to find guilty the killer of a priest.

But the Crown had an ace to play. Sinnisiak had been charged and acquitted only of the murder of Father Rouvière. The Crown had held the charges for the murder of Father LeRoux in abeyance for just this kind of eventuality. When McCaul recovered from the shock of his defeat, he wrote immediately to the deputy minister of justice: "You can easily imagine that I congratulated myself that I had only charged Sinnisiak with the murder of Father Rouvière."

He then applied for a new trial, this time against both Inuit, for the murder of Father LeRoux. Moreover, he applied before the same judge, Horace Harvey, for a change of venue, claiming there was prejudice in Edmonton against the prosecution. Harvey agreed. The trial would commence on August 22, 1917, in Calgary.

In Those Days

Much of the courtroom debate centred on an understanding of what constituted self-defence. McCaul attempted to refute Wallbridge's argument for acquittal on the grounds of self-defence, saying, "My learned friend puts before you the plea of self-defence: that is not the doctrine recognized by British law or by our law. He says a man may kill if he is afraid of being killed. There is no such law in the British Empire. A man may kill only when he is at the moment actually in immediate danger of being killed; but even then he must not kill if there is any method (such as overpowering his assailant) that may obviate the actual necessity of killing. He must not kill except in the last resort." He concluded a lengthy monologue with, "My friend must admit . . . that in the case of a white man, under these circumstances, the jury could not possibly take five minutes [of] consideration before they would bring in a verdict of guilty."

In the face of this, and knowing that the Crown wanted to make an example of the Inuit, Wallbridge adopted a different approach. "It may be suggested to you that these men, whether they are guilty or not, must be made an example of to prevent other incidents of the kind recurring in the wilds, in the Barren lands, at the Arctic Ocean," he began. "That, gentlemen, is not in accordance with our ideas of justice and fair play. If these men are guilty of murder, they should be found guilty of murder and should pay the extreme penalty. If these men are not guilty of murder, then they should be sent to their homes, free. Either they are guilty or they are not guilty. There is no half way measure."

It had already been suggested that, if the two prisoners were convicted, their sentences would be commuted—that they would not pay the price of their lives. Wallbridge thought that that was an incentive for the jury to find the men guilty, and he found that offensive. He continued,

> And it might be suggested to you—it was suggested once—
> that if you find these men guilty they will not be punished by
> the extreme punishment which is meted out to murderers,
> but that their sentence may be commuted, and that they
> will be imprisoned perhaps or dealt with according to the
> ideas of the Minister of Justice. But I say to you that this is a
> matter which you should not take into consideration at all,
> that because a man may not be severely punished is no reason
> why he should be found guilty if he is not guilty. . . . I say that
> if your verdict puts any punishment upon men for reasons
> of supposed policy or any other reasons other than the fact
> that the men are, in your judgment, guilty, then I say that
> that is persecution and not justice.

But McCaul persevered in the argument that Wallbridge found so reprehensible. He responded, "While I submit with some confidence that the evidence not only justifies but requires a verdict of murder, and on this verdict sentence of death must be passed, it seems to me the ideal thing is that this sentence should be commuted to imprisonment for a short term of years."

He went on, "The Government is anxious, as we all can understand, to establish friendly relations with the Eskimo. . . . The Eskimo should be made to realize the white man's justice; he should also be taught that stern justice may, in a proper case, be tempered with mercy. If these men are sent back and imprisoned in the Far North they will be a living object lesson, and they will be able to spread among the tribes of the Arctic the knowledge they have acquired in civilization including some idea, at least, of British law and justice."

And so the argument boiled down to a question of whether the justice system should be used as a tool of government policy. This time, the prosecution got what they wanted. The jury was out for only forty-five minutes and returned with a verdict finding both men guilty of murder, but with a strong recommendation for clemency. What remained was sentencing.

Judge Harvey gave his decision several days later in Edmonton. The law allowed no sentence for murder other than the death penalty. But the jury had strongly urged clemency. Accordingly, the judge sentenced both Inuit to death by hanging. He then explained, through the seventeen-year-old half-Inuit interpreter, Patsy Klengenberg, that the minister "authorizes me to state the sentence will be commuted."

But this would be the last time that Inuit would be given special treatment in the case of murder, for the judge continued, rather simplistically, "Patsy, you might tell them when they get back home, if they do, they must let their people know that if any of them kill any person they will have to suffer death. They know now what our law is."

The death sentences of Sinnisiak and Uluksuk were commuted to life imprisonment at the police detachment in Fort Resolution. They were not confined, but did odd jobs around the post. The police report for 1919 described them as model prisoners who worked willingly and were apparently quite content. In May of that year they were released from custody, and then worked as dog drivers, helping the police to open a new post in the central Arctic at Tree River.

Eventually they returned to their homes, well off in material goods, but arrogant. One police officer said of their return, "They came back with rifles, ammunition, trunks full of white man's clothing, and enough pale-faced cussedness to high-hat the rest of the tribe. Now they're big men among the natives, and some of the others think all they've got to do to have a good time is to stick a knife into someone."

Uluksuk became troublesome; he bullied other natives and was said to be a thief. He bragged that he did not fear the police and "that he would not mind killing a white man, as they [the accused] are only taken outside and given a good time, and then sent back to their own country again." Some reports say that he was killed in 1924 by another native, Ikayena, whom he had been bullying. It turns out that this report was based on confusion with another Inuk with a similar name.

In fact, Uluksuk lived at Bernard Harbour in the late 1920s. The missionary Archibald Lang Fleming met him there is 1928, impoverished, his body racked by tuberculosis. Fleming sent him to the church hospital in Aklavik, but they were unable to provide chronic care. In the summer of 1929 he was sent to Coppermine, where he died in September. Sinnisiak died the following year.

The killing of the Catholic priests and the subsequent trial of the two Inuit has provided rich fodder for writers over the years, and continues to do so. R. G. Moyles published *British Law and Arctic Men* in 1979. McKay Jenkins wrote *Bloody Falls of the Coppermine* in 2005; it's a richer treatment than the earlier book, putting some meat on Moyles's skeletal narrative, which dealt mainly with the trial. In 2010 Keith Ross Leckie fictionalized the whole story in his *Coppermine*.

The most comprehensive academic treatment of the trials is to be found in Edwin Keedy's "A Remarkable Murder Trial,"

In Those Days

published in the *University of Pennsylvania Law Review* in 1951. Keedy, a lawyer, had attended the Edmonton trial. Sidney L. Harring, a law professor in New York, wrote a detailed analysis of the changes to Copper Inuit culture occasioned by the sudden imposition of Canadian law in "The Rich Men of the Country," published in 1989 in the *Ottawa Law Review*.

Playwrights, too, have found this story compelling. In 2010, Thomas Riccio wrote *Ilira*, performed in Dallas, Texas. One of Canada's best-known playwrights, Sharon Pollock, wrote *Kabloona Talk* in 2008; it was performed at Yellowknife's Stuck in a Snowbank Theatre.

Why has the reading public never tired of this story? Perhaps because it has that most North American of themes: a clash of cultures bringing a tragic end. The facts of the case were simple enough, but the interpretation of those facts was more difficult. Of all Inuit in Canada, the changes wrought on Copper Inuit society by their initial encounters with white men were the most sudden. Northerners, especially Inuit, should know this story.

Getting Away with Murder

I n his 1907 book *Nearest the Pole*, the American explorer Robert Peary claimed to have discovered a large land mass north of Ellesmere Island. He named it Crocker Land, after one of his financial backers. Peary faked this discovery—probably to ensure Crocker's continued largesse—for there is no reference to it in his diary. The island simply doesn't exist. But it was very real for the young explorer Donald MacMillan, a participant in Peary's 1908–9 expedition on which Peary claimed to have reached the North Pole. MacMillan believed Peary unquestioningly. In 1913 he returned to the Far North, determined to find and explore Crocker Land. But early in the expedition, he succeeded only in proving its non-existence.

Safely back on Axel Heiberg Island after chasing the mists that were Crocker Land, MacMillan felt a need to salvage something from his journey. He decided to travel to a cape on Ellesmere

In Those Days

Island with Ittukusuk, a hunter and guide, to retrieve a record left there by the Norwegian explorer Otto Sverdrup. He instructed expedition member Fitzhugh Green to travel westward with a native hunter, Piugaattoq, to further explore the coast of Axel Heiberg. But Piugaattoq objected because a storm was brewing. Nevertheless, MacMillan ordered them to leave at once. Piugaattoq reluctantly obeyed.

When the storm hit, Piugaattoq dug a shelter for the two men in a snowbank. Then a snowslide buried Green's sled and killed his dogs. Desperately, Piugaattoq worked to keep a pocket of air open in the cavern he had hollowed out for himself and Green. The American was Green in more than name, but Piugaattoq persevered, and kept him alive.

When the storm abated, Piugaattoq announced that they must return to rendezvous with MacMillan. But Green, despite his inexperience, wanted to continue. The two men argued. A second storm forced them back into the close confines of their refuge.

Finally Piugaattoq had had enough. He told Green that he was turning back. They had only one sled between them, and Piugaattoq forced Green to walk, knowing that the activity was necessary to keep his toes from freezing. Green complained that he could not keep up, but Piugaattoq maintained a steady pace.

Green may have felt that Piugaattoq was abandoning him. On the march, he snatched a rifle from the sled and brandished it in Piugaattoq's direction, ordering the Inuk to follow behind him. When he turned a few minutes later, he saw a frightened Piugaattoq whipping the dogs frantically off in another direction.

Green reported what happened next matter-of-factly in his journal: "I shot once in the air. He did not stop. I then killed him with a shot through the shoulder and another through the head."

Piugaattoq had been a trusted travel companion of Robert Peary on all his polar expeditions. The explorer and anthropologist Knud Rasmussen described him as "a man whom one could trust" and "a comrade who in difficult or dangerous circumstances was ready to make personal sacrifices in order to help and support his companions." Piugaattoq had tried to save Green's life. Green had taken his.

On May 4, 1914, MacMillan recorded the death of Piugaattoq in his diary. Back in America in 1918, he published his story of the Crocker Land Expedition, and wrote dispassionately that "Green, inexperienced in the handling of Eskimos, and failing to understand their motives and temperament, had felt it necessary to shoot his companion."

MacMillan and Green determined to keep the truth from the Inughuit. They told them a half-truth instead. There had been a snowslide, they said, and Piugaattoq had suffocated under it. But Ittukusuk knew the truth as soon as Green returned to MacMillan's camp. He knew a little English, and he had heard the distraught Green blurt out his dismal tale to MacMillan. Ittukusuk told the other Inughuit the truth when they returned to the expedition's headquarters at Etah, on the north Greenland coast. The Inughuit decided not to let on that any of them knew.

Green's actions defy logic. If a man felt he was being abandoned by his guide in unfamiliar and dangerous territory, why shoot the guide? That would simply lessen one's chance of survival. The story makes no sense. Unless there was more to it.

Many of the Inughuit thought that, indeed, there was another reason. Many years ago, when I asked the elders in Qaanaaq why they thought Fitzhugh Green had killed Piugaattoq, they told me that the reason was simple—Green had wanted Piugaattoq's wife,

In Those Days

Aleqasina. She was a strikingly beautiful woman, and had been Peary's mistress until he abandoned her in 1909. Green, the Inughuit believed, desired her. No other reason could explain such an irrational act.

Although MacMillan wrote about it, the murder of Piugaattoq was never investigated. Fitzhugh Green was never punished.

FIGURE 27: Robert Janes, when he was second mate of Bernier's *Arctic*, 1910–11.
SOURCE: J. E. BERNIER / LIBRARY AND ARCHIVES CANADA / PA-061749.

FIGURE 28: Umik, father of Nuqallaq, brought his version of Christianity from Pond Inlet to Igloolik long before the arrival of Christian missionaries.
SOURCE: © THE NATIONAL MUSEUM OF DENMARK, ETHNOGRAPHIC COLLECTIONS.

FIGURE 29: Robert Janes's grave at Pond Inlet.
SOURCE: KENN HARPER COLLECTION.

FIGURE 30: Aatitaaq, Nuqallaq, and Ululijarnaaq (from left to right), the three Inuit accused of the murder of Robert Janes.

SOURCE: LACHLAN T. BURWASH / LIBRARY AND ARCHIVES CANADA / PA-099050.

FIGURE 31: Ataguttiaq, the young wife Nuqallaq left behind when he departed for penitentiary in 1923.

SOURCE: RICHARD S. FINNIE / LIBRARY AND ARCHIVES CANADA / PA-207913.

FIGURE 32: Nuqallaq, before his trial.

SOURCE: L. T. BURWASH / CANADA. DEPT. OF INDIAN AND NORTHERN AFFAIRS / LIBRARY AND ARCHIVES CANADA / C-24524.

FIGURE 33: Nuqallaq at the end of his trial, aboard ship in Pond Inlet, 1923.
SOURCE: THOMAS HENRY TREDGOLD / LIBRARY AND ARCHIVES CANADA / PA-207907.

FIGURE 34: A group of officials outside the courthouse in Pond Inlet, 1923, at the trial for murder of Nuqallaq, Aatitaaq, and Ululijarnaaq.

SOURCE: THOMAS HENRY TREDGOLD / LIBRARY AND ARCHIVES CANADA / PA-187325.

FIGURE 35: Nuqallaq aboard the *Arctic* after his trial for murder, with Judge Rivet and two RCMP officers.

SOURCE: THOMAS HENRY TREDGOLD / LIBRARY AND ARCHIVES CANADA / PA-187327.

FIGURE 36: Nuqallaq aboard ship in 1925, returning from two years' imprisonment in the south. He is in poor health and suffering from tuberculosis.

SOURCE: RICHARD S. FINNIE / LIBRARY AND ARCHIVES CANADA / PA-202074.

FIGURE 37: William Duval as a young man. In his old age he acted as interpreter for the 1923 trial of Nuqallaq in Pond Inlet.

SOURCE: KENN HARPER COLLECTION.

FIGURE 38: Igjugaarjuk, an Inuk deputized as special constable in the search for a murderer.

SOURCE: KENN HARPER COLLECTION, FROM *INTELLECTUAL CULTURE OF THE CARIBOU ESKIMOS: REPORT OF THE FIFTH THULE EXPEDITION, 1921—24*, VOL. VII, BY KNUD RASMUSSEN.

FIGURE 39: Atqaaralaaq, wife of Igjugaarjuk.
SOURCE: KENN HARPER COLLECTION, FROM *INTELLECTUAL CULTURE OF THE CARIBOU ESKIMOS: REPORT OF THE FIFTH THULE EXPEDITION, 1921–24*, VOL. VII, BY KNUD RASMUSSEN.

FIGURE 40: Alikomiak at Herschel Island, 1923. He was hanged on February 1, 1924, convicted of murder.

SOURCE: GLENBOW ARCHIVES, PA-3886-29-5.

FIGURE 41: RCMP officers with the hangman, Mr. Gill (second from right), Herschel Island, 1923.
SOURCE: GLENBOW ARCHIVES, PA-3886-29-3.

FIGURE 42: Portrait of Knud Rasmussen
by Godthaabs Fotografiske, before
the start of the Fifth Thule Expedition.
SOURCE: GLENBOW ARCHIVES, PA-3886-28.

KNOW YE

The King of the Land commands you, saying:

'THOU SHALT DO NO MURDER"

Why does he speak thus?

Long ago our God made the world, and He owns the world.

The people also He made, and He owns them.

The King of the land is commanded by God to protect the people well.

The white people and Indians and Eskimos have him for their ruler. He is their ruler, therefore he commands, saying:

"THOU SHALT DO NO MURDER"

But if a man kills a man, the King sends his servants, the police, to take and kill the murderer.

But ye do not kill the murderer, nor cause him to be killed. This only the King's servants, the police, ought to do

But when a man commits murder, at once tell the King's servants, the police, and they will take and bind the murderer and the ruler will judge him.

Thus our God commands us so that you are to follow the King's command

DUNCAN C. SCOTT,
In Charge of Indian Affairs, Ottawa, Canada

GEORGE, R.I

FIGURE 43: "Thou Shalt Do No Murder," a poster distributed to trading and police posts throughout the Canadian North in 1925.
SOURCE: KENN HARPER COLLECTION.

FIGURE 44: Peter Sala, left, one of the perpetrators of the Belcher Island murders in 1942.
SOURCE: FREDERICA KNIGHT FONDS / AVATAQ CULTURAL INSTITUTE / FK-011.

FIGURE 45: Mina, the sister of Peter Sala, was responsible for the deaths of a number of women and children during the Belcher Island murders.
SOURCE: FREDERICA KNIGHT FONDS / AVATAQ CULTURAL INSTITUTE / FK-009.

FIGURE 46: Angulaalik, a successful independent trader in Kitikmeot Region, and his family.
SOURCE: S. J. BAILEY / LIBRARY AND ARCHIVES CANADA / PA-175729.

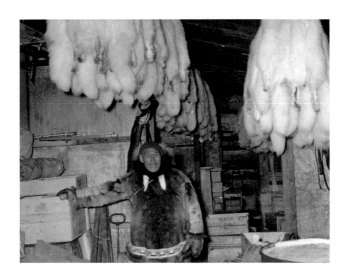

FIGURE 47: Angulaalik and his furs.
SOURCE: J. C. JACKSON / CANADA. DEPT. OF INDIAN AND NORTHERN AFFAIRS / LIBRARY AND ARCHIVES CANADA / E010674364.

FIGURE 48: Captain and Mrs. C. T. Pedersen. Captain Pedersen set up Angulaalik as his local trader when Canadian law prohibited Pedersen, an American, from trading directly with Inuit. SOURCE: GLENBOW ARCHIVES, PA-3886-65-20.

FIGURE 49: Isaac Shooyook, the oldest person elected to the Nunavut legislature in its history. Shooyook was tried for murder in 1965. SOURCE: COURTESY OF LEGISLATIVE ASSEMBLY OF NUNAVUT.

Blood on the Snow

Robert Janes's Last Journey

Robert Janes was born on the Gooseberry Islands near Glovertown, Newfoundland, and first travelled to the Arctic as second mate on the Canadian government ship *Arctic*, under the famous Captain Bernier, in 1910. From the English term "second mate" came his Inuktitut name, Sakirmiaq. In 1912 he returned north on an unsuccessful summer expedition in search of gold at Pond Inlet. Finally, he came back for the third time in 1916 and established a trading post west of Pond Inlet at Patricia River. But competition was intense. Two rivals already had trading posts nearby.

Janes quarrelled with the Inuit and with the rival traders. In particular, he quarrelled with an Inuit leader, Nuqallaq. At first they were at odds over a woman. Nuqallaq's wife, Ullatitaq, tired

In Those Days

of her husband's cruel beatings, had committed suicide. Janes had left his wife, Leah, and twelve children behind in St. John's. Both men decided that they wanted an attractive young woman, Kalluk, who was married to Inuutiq, who worked for Janes. In fact, Janes, Kalluk, and Inuutiq all lived together in a ménage à trois in Janes's small shack. But Nuqallaq happened by from time to time when Janes was away. This situation eventually sorted itself out when Nuqallaq took another woman, Ataguttiaq, as his wife.

But Janes had problems with other Inuit over trade. He had liberally advanced goods on credit in the early days of his trading post, but eventually ran out of trade goods. He solved that problem by simply extorting furs from Inuit at gunpoint, becoming a very unpopular man in the process. But his life took a decided turn for the worse in 1919, when his rival, Captain Henry Toke Munn—Kapitaikuluk ("the little captain")—arrived with supplies for his own post, and news for Janes. His backer in St. John's had sold the ship. No relief was coming for Robert Janes. Munn and Janes were unable to agree on the terms of passage south, and Munn departed, leaving Janes behind.

This departure left Robert Janes in northern Baffin Island to prepare for his fourth winter in the Arctic. One other white man shared the district with him, a Peterhead man, George Diament.

That winter, Janes concocted a desperate scheme to reach the south and home. With one native, Uuttukuttuk, as his guide and driver, he would go west through Eclipse Sound, north through Navy Board Inlet, and into Lancaster Sound to round the northern tip of Borden Peninsula. From there he would head south through Admiralty Inlet to Arctic Bay, where he hoped to meet natives and secure from them dog food sufficient to allow him to reach the Inuit camp at Igloolik in Foxe Basin. He would secure more food from natives there and continue on to Repulse Bay. There he would dismiss Uuttukuttuk and hire another guide to take him that same spring along the Keewatin coast as far as Churchill, and from there to the terminus of the Hudson Bay railroad. He would travel by train to Winnipeg. From there he would continue on to St. John's. There he would charter a vessel to go back north to Patricia River to bring out the furs that he was leaving behind.

His journey began on February 24, 1920. Janes kept a daily diary on this, his last trip. Called "Record of Expedition to Hudson's [*sic*] Bay," it is for the most part a lucid recording of the journey, an optimistic account of a difficult trip on which temperatures reached as low as minus forty-five degrees Fahrenheit. Until the last two entries, there is no reference to trouble with any Inuit and no hint of the ill temper that had marred his previous relations with them. The diary describes starkly and sparely Robert Janes's attempt to escape from his Arctic hell:

Monday, February 24

Calm and clear. Thermometer 36 below. Left station outward bound to try and reach civilization. Team eleven dogs, load about 800 pounds. Snow deep and going slow. At 3 p.m. cached half and sleighed till 11 p.m. when we reached south-west Bylot and put up for night in driver's igloo.

That morning Robert Janes bid farewell to his mistress, Kalluk, and her husband, Inuutiq. Kalluk was heavy with Janes's child, a child whom Inuutiq would have the responsibility of feeding and raising, and Janes knew that he would never see her again. It mattered little. He was on his way home to Leah and the large family that awaited his return in St. John's. He had picked probably the coldest time of the year to begin such a journey. But the trip would be a long one, and there was no time to spare by waiting for warmer weather.

On their third day of travel, Janes and Uuttukuttuk rounded the southwestern tip of Bylot Island and entered Navy Board Inlet. There they met another native, Kaukuarjuk. There was no trouble between Janes and the Inuk—in fact, Kaukuarjuk provided the trader with some caribou meat—but there was a portent of things to come. Janes raised the subject of his old enemy, Nuqallaq, and told Kaukuarjuk that Nuqallaq was no good, an indication that Janes continued to bear malice against the man who had slept with his mistress two years earlier. Ironically, when Kaukuarjuk, more lightly loaded and able to travel faster, left Janes and headed north, his destination was Nuqallaq's camp.

Uuttukuttuk's wife, who had accompanied her husband and Janes this far, wanted to continue with her husband on his long journey. Supplies of food in her camp were scarce near the end of a long winter of darkness, and her husband had little to leave for her. Native hunting patterns had been so severely disrupted by the Inuit's need to trap foxes for the competing traders in the district that privation was often the result. But Janes needed speed on this trip, and could not be encumbered with a family accompanying his guide. Janes prevailed, and the following day the two men travelled on alone.

Travel was slow. By the end of February, the party was still in Navy Board Inlet. The trip so far had been plagued by bad weather. It was bitterly cold—minus forty-five at one point. Still, it was early, and Janes was filled with optimism. His diary entry for the last day of February conveys no hint of despair:

Saturday, February 29

Strong westerly wind with heavy drift over ice. In Narrows about 6 miles to the north of us it blew a gale all day, too much so to make a move. The day was bitterly cold, 35 below. Sent native to hunt. Have returned at 4 p.m. with three partridge which gave us a good supper. We have a very good stock of meat, enough to last as far as Arctic Bay, Admiralty Inlet if favourable weather prevails. Not so bad in igloo considering the frost outside. Night fine, wind moderating, all well.

Away goes February. Taboutie.

Janes's "Taboutie" is the Inuktitut word *tavvauvutit*—"goodbye," with which he bid farewell to the month of February. To Inuit, this month was traditionally called *avunnivik*—"the month of miscarriages." Although the sun had returned over the horizon in the High Arctic, this was nonetheless the coldest month of the year. In particularly bad years, caribou often suffered miscarriages about this time.

Dog-team travel provides plenty of time for reflection. And Robert Janes had plenty to think about. His relations with many Inuit had been rocky. He had bullied and threatened some, and extorted furs from a number of them after his trade goods had run out. He looked forward to leaving the Arctic and getting back to St. John's and the family he had not seen for almost four years. His wife was caring for their dozen children. He thought fondly of them all and had nicknames for most. Among them were two boys who were his pride and joy, Ambrose and Eggerton—Janes called them "Ham and Egg." He was leaving behind Kalluk, the woman he had lived with (along with her real husband) for over three years, and who was pregnant with his child. And there was also an eight-year-old girl, Ataguttaq, whom he had sired on his first trip to the Arctic. He recognized her as his daughter and often gave her presents.

On March 4, ten days into his desperate bid to reach the south, he passed Adams Island in Lancaster Sound. Although he saw no sign of Inuit, a group was camped there, perhaps on the opposite side of the island from which he passed. This was Nuqallaq's camp. Kaukuarjuk had warned Nuqallaq that Janes was heading in this direction and that he was still obsessed with his dislike for him. Nuqallaq still feared the unstable trader and had decided that it was better for Janes to pass without meeting him. In doing so, Nuqallaq demonstrated the same tactic of avoidance of confrontation that he had shown in earlier years when experiencing difficult relations with white men. It was a display not of cowardice, but of common sense.

Janes and Uuttukuttuk left Navy Board Inlet and skirted the coast of Baffin Island's Borden Peninsula along Lancaster Sound, which marked the eastern entrance to the fabled Northwest Passage. Its ice was often unstable, but the landfast ice close to shore, on which Janes and his partner travelled, formed a stable platform for safe travel at this time of year.

Janes hoped to meet Inuit near Arctic Bay, from whom he could get fresh seal meat to feed his hungry dogs. He sent Uuttukuttuk on ahead with a lightly loaded sled to see if the Inuit were still at Strathcona Sound. Janes spent the night alone, drying his clothes and tending to his gear. The temperature was minus twenty-five. He noted in his journal, "Today makes 15 days and not at my destination yet, the longest trip here during my stay in this land. Night fine. All well."

When Uuttukuttuk returned, it was with news that confirmed Janes's fears. There were no Inuit at Strathcona Sound, but there were sled tracks, and they indicated that the natives had all headed west. Now Janes faced uncertainty as to whether to continue on to Arctic Bay or make a long diversion northwest to Cape Crauford. He could not be sure of encountering any Inuit at Arctic Bay, for the winter there had been severe and food had been in short supply. He felt it more likely that the whole population had re-located to Cape Crauford—Kangiq, as they called it—a favoured spring sealing area on the western shore of the mouth of Admiralty Inlet. It was important that Janes meet a large group of Inuit soon, for he needed more dog food for his dash to Igloolik, three hundred miles to the south, the next location where he could be assured of meeting natives. If the Inuit had moved on to Cape Crauford, then he must follow, even though the diversion would add days to a trip already behind schedule. On March 10, he made his decision. His diary records the events of that day.

Tuesday, March 10

Cape Crauford. Wind strong westerly and bitterly cold. Driver returned from the west at 6 a.m. after being all day and night going and coming. He saw no natives but saw plenty of sleigh tracks. We picked up our gear and got away from igloo at 9 a.m. This has been one of the coldest days I have ever spent on a sleigh. Pretty tough to keep from freezing. As it was, I got my nose frozen. Half way to Cape Crauford we cached our outfit. Dogs pretty tired. We made poor progress. At 6 p.m. we arrived at native colony three miles off Cape Crauford and were glad to get into a native igloo. Fortunately I picked a warm one. Several are away down

In Those Days

in bottom of inlet. I may see them later on. Night fine. All well. Thermometer 38 below.

When Janes and Uuttukuttuk arrived at Cape Crauford, seven native families were camped there. They were there for the spring seal hunt, so their camp was a few miles offshore on the landfast ice. Four feet thick at this time of year, this ice would form a surface for travelling and camping until June. The sun had returned to northern Baffin Island in early February, and the amount of light was increasing daily. The evening light lasted until about ten o'clock, and dawn came in the wee hours of the morning. Janes and his guide moved into Paumik's snowhouse and were made welcome. The trader intended to spend only a few days at this camp before continuing south.

The following day, however, more Inuit arrived at the camp. Among them was Nuqallaq.

Janes's intended quick stop at Cape Crauford stretched into a number of days. During this time, his behaviour became quite irrational. Convinced that many of the hunters owed him for trade, he began to threaten them. He would, he claimed, kill the Inuit and their dogs if they did not hand over their furs. The men of the camp held a meeting. If Janes's behaviour did not improve, someone would have to kill him. As a natural leader, that man would have to be Nuqallaq.

Morning dawned clear and cold on Sunday, March 15. Robert Janes began his sixth day at Cape Crauford. He was the most northerly white man in Canada and the only non-native in a hunting camp of nineteen Inuit men, some accompanied by their wives and children.

The Inuit men went hunting, as usual. When they returned,

they heard that Janes had continued his bizarre behaviour, and they knew that they could no longer postpone the inevitable.

That night, Nuqallaq hid himself behind Ataguttaaluk's snowhouse, while Aatitaaq stood beside its entry. Maniq positioned a *qamutiik* (dog sled) upright beside Nuqallaq to conceal him. Nuqallaq was the only man carrying a gun. With everyone in position, Ululijarnaaq went to Paumik's igloo and asked Janes to come out. Some Inuit had fox pelts for him, he told the trader.

Janes didn't bother with his parka. He would be warm enough in his heavy red woollen shirt and thick vest. Caribou-skin pants and boots covered his lower body. He bent his lanky frame through the low doorway and stepped into the chill spring night. Ululijar naaq followed him out. Maniq whispered loudly to Nuqallaq that Janes was outside. The trader strode straight along the path in the direction of Nuqallaq's snowhouse. Ululijarnaaq, missing his cue, suddenly told the trader to stop, then, realizing that he was not yet in Nuqallaq's sight, just as abruptly told him to carry on. Janes walked a little farther, a target growing larger and closer. The hunter aimed nervously and fired. The shot missed. Janes, suddenly angry and afraid, cried out in English, but the Inuit could not understand what he said. He kept walking. He couldn't tell where the sound had come from, but he recognized it as a rifle shot. He looked around, confused and frightened, and recognized Nuqallaq. Not realizing that he was staring into the face of his executioner, he called out to him, "Nuqallaq *uvvaa* (Nuqallaq, here)!" Terror gripped him as he begged Nuqallaq to help him. Nuqallaq fired again, and this time the bullet ripped through the vest and woollen shirt and tore through his flesh above the hip. Aatitaaq then ran up behind Janes, took hold of him above the hips, and pushed him along, until Janes tripped over a qamutiik. Aatitaaq gave him a final push and he fell to the ground.

Blood oozed from under Janes's clothing, and a crimson stain crept darkly across the hard-packed snow. The trader tried to get up, but he could only rise enough to place his weight on one elbow as he cried out in pain and fear.

Some of the men came from their snowhouses and congregated around Janes. They stood expressionless over the fallen trader, like official witnesses at an execution. No one spoke. There was nothing left to say, to Janes or to each other. Words had already failed. The only sounds were the cries of the man they knew as Sakirmiaq as he thrashed about in agony and in the certain knowledge of his impending death.

Nuqallaq gazed down at his old tormentor. Janes searched the faces above him for that of his nemesis. Their eyes met. In that instant, fear and resignation melded into a mutual acceptance of the inevitable. Nuqallaq raised the rifle slowly but without hesitation. The width of a qamutiik separated him from Janes. A final shot seared cleanly through the trader's head. The bullet entered his skull above the left ear and exited behind the right ear into the snow.

Three years later, Nuqallaq, Ululijarnaaq, and Aatitaaq would stand trial for murder.

The Trial
and Punishment
of Nuqallaq

I n August of 1921, Staff Sergeant Alfred Herbert Joy reached
Pond Inlet on the Hudson's Bay Company ship *Baychimo*.
The Bay was establishing its most northerly fur trading
post, and the Royal Canadian Mounted Police was simultane-
ously establishing a police detachment.

Headquarters' instructions to Joy were all-encompassing: "A
detachment is to be established at Pond Inlet, Baffin Island, and you
have been selected to take charge of it. You have been appointed a
justice of the peace in the Northwest Territories, in which Baffin
Island is situated; a coroner, a special officer of the customs, and a
postmaster of a post office located at Pond Inlet."

On December 26, on the first of his many famous Arctic patrols,

In Those Days

Joy, travelling with a group of Inuit, disinterred Robert Janes's body from its crude rock grave on the shores of Brodeur Peninsula and brought it back to Pond Inlet. On January 21, 1922, he conducted an autopsy.

Justice had to be carried out properly, thought Joy. That meant forms to be filled out, informations to be sworn, and notices to be served. With only four white men in the district, Joy arranged a circus of formalities to deal with the trappings of white man's law. On January 23, he arranged that Wilfred Caron, an employee of another fur-trading company, would appear in his presence and swear an Information to Hold Inquest. Joy then swore Wilfred Parsons of the Hudson's Bay Company in as special constable, so that Parsons could then issue a Warrant to Summon a Jury to Joy himself, who then duly served a Summons to Jury to each of Caron, Parsons, and the latter's assistant, Gaston Herodier.

Tellingly, Joy noted in his official report that these three were "all the competent men available as jurors." Joy had given no thought to including Inuit on the jury. Parsons, although now a member of the jury, was still a special constable, and in that capacity he next served a Summons to Witness to Coroner Joy and to the three Inuit men, Urulu, Tuurngaq, and Ululijarnaaq, who had accompanied Joy in recovering the body of the deceased.

On the same day that this flurry of paperwork was handled, the coroner's inquest opened at four thirty in the afternoon. James Tooktosina, an Inuk from Labrador in the service of the Hudson's Bay Company, served as interpreter. With few buildings available, the inquest was held in the living room of the trading post. Other Inuit witnesses had to be called, and there were numerous adjournments ordered by Coroner Joy so that he, in his role as Staff Sergeant Joy, police officer, could summon the additional witnesses to testify. In fact, the inquest went on well into February. The Inuit who were summoned told what they knew of the events, and everything was duly interpreted for the benefit of the white men, who scrupulously noted everything said.

One can only wonder what impression this formality, this insistence on written testimony, this obsession with the trappings of southern justice, had on the Inuit. They cannot have understood the role that Joy, claiming to represent a country called Canada, would play in their lives and futures, and how he was different from the new traders, Parsons and Herodier. For now, they were all Qallunaat (white people), and the Inuit gave them all Inuktitut names. Parsons they dubbed Nujaqanngittuq, the bald one. Herodier became known as Ataataluk, the poor father. But Alfred Herbert Joy was simply called Saarjan, an attempt to pronounce his rank rather than his name.

On February 10, the jury retired and returned with its verdict in twenty minutes. It read:

> That the said Robert Janes was shot to death on or about the end of March in the year one thousand nine hundred and twenty, the precise date being to the jurors unknown, at Cape Crauford in the North-west Territories. And that the cause of his death was that Nuqallaq alias Qiugaarjuk, Eskimo, did feloniously and of his malice aforethought kill and murder the said Robert Janes by shooting him through the body and head with a rifle, from which he instantly died.
>
> And do so further say that Ululijarnaaq, Eskimo, and Aatitaaq, Eskimo, did feloniously and of their malice aforethought aid and abet the said Nuqallaq alias Qiugaarjuk in committing the said felonious act.

In Those Days

With a verdict in hand, Coroner Joy dismissed the jury the next day. Then, that same day, Parsons, acting again in his role as special constable, laid an Information and Complaint before Joy, who now acted not as police officer, but as justice of the peace. The complaint was against Nuqallaq, Ululijarnaaq, and Aatitaaq for the murder of Robert Janes, contrary to section 263 of the Criminal Code. Later that day, Joy, still acting as justice of the peace, issued a Warrant to Apprehend for each of the three Inuit; he noted that these warrants were issued and "retained by me." In fact, Joy as justice of the peace had directed Joy as police officer to arrest the three men. They were later tried for murder. This would be the first murder trial in what would become Nunavut.

Finally, in 1923, the paraphernalia of a foreign justice system had been put in place, the ship bringing strange men with new ideas from the South had arrived, and the trial was ready to begin on Saturday, August 25, 1923, at ten fifteen in the morning in the police detachment. It was attended by almost all of the ship's personnel, and by "as many Eskimos as could be crowded into the building." This court was conducted with all the pomp and ceremony that a murder case would have had in southern Canada, "in civilization," as the police described it.

The judge made a few introductory remarks to the Inuit, translated by the interpreter, the well-known William Duval. He explained the purpose of the trial, and assured them of "justice and fairplay"; he told them that "the proceedings were exactly in accordance with the customs of civilization, and stated that had a white man killed an Eskimo the proceedings would have been exactly the same." The indictment was read to the three accused, all charged with murder. They entered their pleas: not guilty. The jury members were called and sworn in—all white men from the ship's crew.

The prosecution began its case against the three accused, who had no way of comprehending the gravity of the charges against them. A cultural gap of more than just language separated them from these newcomers.

That first day, court sat late into the night, but it did not sit the following day. According to law, it could not sit on a Sunday. The white men spent the day sleeping and resting, the Inuit in "merry-making and dancing." It was unusual for this many Inuit to be gathered together in one place, and they made the most of it, visiting, gossiping, and catching up on news of far-off friends and relatives.

The prosecution continued its case on Monday with more testimony from Inuit who recounted the details of the tragic events that had led to Janes's killing. The lengthy trial record does not contain verbatim transcripts, but rather a summary of the proceedings and evidence. It is apparent that the Inuit respondents were all answering a standard series of questions.

On Tuesday afternoon, the defence began calling its witnesses. The court record states, strangely, that Tellier, attorney for the accused, declared that "the same evidence should apply to the three accused, inasmuch as it can apply." This is a strange tactic for a defence attorney to use, and does not augur well for the accused. But things quickly got stranger. Incredibly, the first witness Tellier called for the defence was the court interpreter, William Duval—who would therefore be tasked with interpreting his own testimony. That afternoon the defence called other witnesses. The trial continued for a number of days. Eventually, two of the accused, Nuqallaq and Aatitaaq, testified in their own defence.

On the morning of August 30, both sides wrapped up their

cases. Crown Prosecutor Falardeau pressed for a conviction of all three men. He pointed out that "in civilization, he would ask for a verdict of murder, but taking into consideration the ignorance of the prisoners, he only asked for a verdict of manslaughter." He told the jury that they could recommend the accused to the clemency of the court.

The judge then addressed the jury. His biases were obvious. He was lavish in his praise for the RCMP. The jury was out for only thirty minutes, returning at 11:50 a.m. with its verdicts. Nuqallaq and Ululijarnaaq were both found guilty of manslaughter, but with a recommendation for clemency for Ululijarnaaq. Aatitaaq was found not guilty.

The judge passed sentence immediately. Nuqallaq was sentenced to ten years' imprisonment with hard labour in Stony Mountain Penitentiary in Manitoba. Ululijarnaaq was given two years' imprisonment with hard labour at the police guardroom in Pond Inlet. Aatitaaq was discharged.

The judge explained to the prisoners "the enormity of their crime and impressed upon them and upon the other natives present the fact that he considered the sentences very lenient and that any future occurrences of a similar kind would be dealt with much more severely."

Nuqallaq was led away immediately "through a gazing crowd of his own people, without being given a chance to communicate with any of them." He was taken aboard the *Arctic*. The ship left that night. Before its departure, nineteen-year-old Ataguttiaq went aboard to bid her husband farewell. She was a young woman and scarcely understood what was happening. She wept. Nuqallaq remained unperturbed. Perhaps he was simply trying to put a brave face on his desperate situation.

The ship departed for a land Nuqallaq had never seen. His sentence had begun.

Imprisonment was hard on Nuqallaq. His half-sister, Agatha Tongak, summed it up succinctly: "He worked so hard that he got tuberculosis." He found solace in his Bible, written in Inuktitut syllabics. He spoke only a little English. He was very much alone.

Less than six months after Nuqallaq's imprisonment began in Stony Mountain, he received a surprise visitor. It was none other than Captain Munn, a trader who had operated a post near Pond Inlet, in competition with Robert Janes, and whom Nuqallaq knew well. Munn found Nuqallaq much thinner than when he had last seen him in 1922, and the native complained that his food was "no good." Nuqallaq sweated through the whole interview and Munn thought that the heat of the jail was too much for him to bear.

Munn immediately began to press Ottawa to release Nuqallaq early under a Ticket of Leave and send him back to Pond Inlet to work for the police there. Munn thought Nuqallaq had lost the will to live and was not likely to survive a second year in jail.

This put another series of bureaucratic procedures in motion. Munn's claims had to be investigated and the old trader's veracity considered. The opinion of the RCMP was solicited, and they were very much against Nuqallaq's early release, as were most of the bureaucrats at the Department of the Interior.

Then, in March of 1924, Nuqallaq's health suddenly took a turn for the worse. He was admitted to hospital with influenza, and an examination showed the presence of tuberculosis bacilli. His weight had dropped to 146 pounds. The prison doctor thought that "he will continue to fail very rapidly if still confined in the

Penitentiary. Were he living in the open air night and day, he would have a better chance of recovery."

Finally, in the late spring of 1925, the governor general granted a Ticket of Leave to allow Nuqallaq to return home on the ship that summer.

Aboard the *Arctic*, Nuqallaq was housed in one of the whaleboats on deck. The fresh air on the early part of the trip brought a marked improvement to his health. Off Cape Mercy, with the ship in the pack, he even went for a walk on the ice. But by early August he was sick again, with pain in his chest, and coughing. The doctor diagnosed pleurisy. He was given eggs, milk, and whisky as treatment, but soon became impatient for heavier food and ate ravenously for a number of nights. He despaired of reaching Pond Inlet alive, and convinced himself that the inlet would be full of ice and prevent his return.

Finally, on September 3, the ship reached Pond Inlet. Nuqallaq dressed up in a white man's suit for his return. He went ashore and was greeted by his young and attractive wife, Ataguttiaq. His sole possessions were $3.15, a ring with five stones for his wife, his Ticket of Leave, and his Inuktitut Bible, which he is said to have carried everywhere with him. The government officials aboard the *Arctic* watched Nuqallaq's reunion with his people and reported that "there was no demonstration when he arrived. He was still considered in the bad books of the white man because of his crime."

When Nuqallaq was taken away in the fall of 1923, he of course left Ataguttiaq behind. She had begun a relationship with a young policeman, Ernie Friel, called Makkulaaq by the Inuit because he was the youngest of four officers stationed at Pond Inlet. He was an active young man, who learned to drive a dog team and maintained a trap line on Bylot Island. Friel's relationship with Ataguttiaq was open and known to all in the district. In February 1925, Ataguttiaq bore Friel's child, a boy named Arnakallak. He remained with his mother for only the first three days of his life, then was given to his grandparents, Qamaniq and Makpainuk, to be raised. Nuqallaq learned of the existence of this little boy as soon as he arrived. It didn't matter. He accepted him. The important thing was that he was home.

One of Nuqallaq's first desires was for a good feed of seal meat. The police provided him a tent and did what they could to make his quarters comfortable. After his meal, he went to bed and was still there when the ship departed for the south. In fact, he was dying. The ship's doctor noted, "He was expectorating some blood. . . . The prognosis is grave."

During the next two months, Nuqallaq hunted seals sporadically. In November he worked for some days for the Hudson's Bay Company, then left with his wife and others for Arctic Sound to hunt. One day, his hunting partner, Kipumii, fell through the ice. Nuqallaq was unable to reach him, and shouted at the top of his voice for help. Others heard him and saved Kipumii, but Inuit believe the exertion his shouting put on his badly damaged lungs worsened his health.

The police visited Nuqallaq at Emerson Island in the middle of November and found him sick and confined to a damp, cold snowhouse. On December 5, he died. He was buried at Iqaluit in Tay Sound.

Judge Rivet's sentence had been a death sentence after all.

Deputizing a Murderer

In the summer of 1922, the great explorer and ethnologist Knud Rasmussen was travelling in the interior of the Keewatin region on the most famous of his Arctic travels, the Fifth Thule Expedition. Greenlandic was his native tongue. Canadian Inuit called him Kunu.

In a small camp of only three tents at the lake known as Hikoligjuaq, he found a man he had been hoping to meet, a man about whom he had heard a great deal. This was Igjugaarjuk—the name means "the little testicle"—a man held in high esteem by his countrymen.

To prove his worth, Igjugaarjuk immediately handed Kunu a document that bore the seal of the Canadian government, issued to him by one Alfred E. Reames, an officer of the Royal Canadian Mounted Police acting as justice of the peace. Reames had been at the same lake on April 8, 1921, on a manhunt for an Inuk suspected of murder, and had himself sought the assistance of Igjugaarjuk. The document that Reames issued him was captioned "Appointment as Special Constable" and addressed "To whom it may concern." It read as follows:

"This is to certify that the bearer, one Ed-jo-a-juk, Padlermiut Escimo [sic], of Lake She-ko-lig-you-ak, North West Territories, Canada, has this day been appointed by me . . . one of His Majesty's Justices of the Peace, in and for the North West Territories, for the purposes of apprehending and bringing to justice, one Ouangwak, Padlermiut Escimo [sic], wanted on two charges of murder, and for whose arrest warrants have been duly issued. The said Ed-jo-a-juk to have all the privileges, rights and appertenances [sic] duly connected with the said office of Special Constable in the Territories."

Reames had, in effect, deputized Igjugaarjuk.

Kunu was immediately impressed by this man. He described him as wise, independent, and intelligent, and thought that he exercised a great deal of authority over his fellows. In a land where there were far fewer women than men, as a result of female infanticide, he demonstrated his might and authority by having two wives. Kunu spent considerable time at Igjugaarjuk's camp and collected a number of legends from him. On this expedition, Kunu was to eventually travel as far as Siberia, meeting all the groups of Inuit along his sled route. So it is high praise indeed when he describes Igjugaarjuk in this manner: "Of all the people I have met on the long stretch between Greenland and Siberia, he occupies an outstanding place among all the prominent Eskimos."

But, despite Igjugaarjuk's qualities of leadership, Kunu found it amazing that he was able to brandish a paper naming him as a special constable of the RCMP. For what Kunu already knew was that Igjugaarjuk himself was guilty of a mass murder.

Kunu tells the tale succinctly:

"As a young man Igjugaarjuk had been in love with a woman named Kibgarjuk, but her family were opposed to the match. When he heard later that they thought of giving her to another man, he turned up unexpectedly one day, with his eldest brother, Harpik, at the entrance to the snow house where Kibgarjuk lived, and from there shot down her father, mother, two brothers with their respective wives and finally, when Kibgarjuk had become alone, sprang in, carried her off and married her."

It is doubtful that the policeman, Reames, knew anything of Igjugaarjuk's past. It is equally doubtful that Igjugaarjuk put much energy into bringing the accused, Ouangwak, into custody.

The Only Inuit Hanged in Canada

In 1920, word reached Constable W. A. Doak at the newly established Tree River RCMP detachment in the western part of today's Kitikmeot Region that five Inuit had been murdered on Kent Peninsula. Doak set out to investigate. He discovered that a number of the reported killings had occurred because of domestic disputes. One man, Tatamigana, had killed two other men, then together with his nephew, Alikomiak, a young man about sixteen or eighteen years of age, killed a third man, Pugnana. Doak arrested both men and took them back to Tree River.

The officer took a personal interest in young Alikomiak and made him a kind of servant. Alikomiak cleaned the house, looked after Doak's clothing, and did other menial work. On April 1, Doak rose from bed and called for his young servant to bring him his sealskin boots. Alikomiak threw them to him, but Doak threw them back, telling him that the soles were not supple enough and needed to be chewed. This was woman's work, as Alikomiak well knew. He also spilled the slop bucket, and was chastised and thrown out of the house. Alikomiak brooded throughout the day. That night he went to a storehouse and came out with a rifle and four bullets. He entered the house and, with no warning, shot Doak in the upper leg. He then sat down and calmly watched as the officer bled to death.

Otto Binder, a trader who lived nearby, was in the habit of making a morning call on Doak. The next morning, when Binder was halfway to the police post, Alikomiak broke out a windowpane and fired one shot through the trader's heart. He died instantly. Alikomiak then went to Binder's house and told the trader's Inuit common-law wife what he had done, and announced that he was going to the camp nearby to kill all the other white men. One of the Inuit secretly sent his son ahead to warn the whites, and Sergeant Woolams arrested Alikomiak, who had just finished boasting that killing a white man was as easy as killing a ptarmigan.

That summer Alikomiak and Tatamigana were both taken to Herschel Island aboard a Hudson's Bay Company ship. They would be tried for murder. But the policy-makers in Ottawa had made a strategic decision. Sinnisiak and Uluksuk, two Inuit who had earlier been tried for the killing of two priests, had been treated leniently, to no avail; the leniency shown them had not deterred further murders. This time there would be no leniency. Tatamigana and Alikomiak would be found guilty and hanged.

The RCMP wrote to the Department of the Interior in 1922,

recommending that a trial be held in the Arctic, where Inuit could see first-hand the workings of white man's justice. T. L. Cory, solicitor for the Northwest Territories Branch, concurred when he wrote, "The advantage in having the accused murderers tried in their own country among their own people, will be to bring home to the natives the result of their comrades' actions. . . . As kindness has failed in the past I strongly recommend that the law should take its course and those Eskimos found guilty of murder should be hanged in a place where natives will see and recognize the outcome of taking another life." Amazingly, only a few months later, Cory was appointed to defend the very men he had thought should be hanged.

Judge Lucien Dubuc of Edmonton, a stipendiary magistrate of the Northwest Territories, was assigned to carry out the trial at Herschel Island. The jurors were all white.

Tatamigana was convicted of the murder of Ikpukwak, one of the five men whose murders had touched off this chain of events, but the six-man jury recommended mercy. Both Tatamigana and Alikomiak were next convicted of killing Pugnana and sentenced to death. Finally Alikomiak was tried for the murder of Constable Doak. The trial occurred on July 18, 1923, and took only one day. The verdict was guilty.

But the trial, regardless of the guilt of Alikomiak, was a sham. The lumber to build the gallows accompanied the judge's party when it left Edmonton. A hangman travelled incognito with the court party. But most damning is the existence of a telegram from the deputy minister of justice to Judge Dubuc *before* the judge's departure from Edmonton for Herschel Island. It reads, "Eskimo trials you should consult police authorities as to the date and place of execution, understand they favour Herschel Island."

In Those Days

So the authorities had decided before the trial that a verdict of guilty would be the result, and that the inevitable sentence of death would result in a hanging.

Judge Dubuc waited some weeks before actually passing sentence. By the time he did, the gallows had already been constructed in the Herschel Island bone house, an old building for drying whalebone left over from whaling days. After sentence was passed, Alikomiak, grinning and uncomprehending, left the prisoner's dock and handed the judge a cigarette as he passed the bench.

The executions took place on February 1, 1924. At dawn on that date, Alikomiak and Tatamigana were led to the gallows. They appeared to be in high spirits and shook hands with everyone there. Alikomiak offered the executioner a cigarette and gave a small ivory carving to the wife of the police superintendent. But once he stood on the scaffold, his final words were a declaration that the police had long been the enemies of his people. Both men were buried in the graveyard at Herschel Island.

A storm of protest in southern Canada had resulted from the convictions of the two Inuit. It was led by Bishop J. R. Lucas of the Church of England, who first brought to the attention of the public that the court party had been accompanied by a hangman and had carried lumber for the construction of a gallows, and that even the graves for the reception of the bodies of Alikomiak and Tatamigana had been dug before sentence was passed. Lucas painted a pathetic scene of what had taken place in the Herschel Island courtroom: only a dozen spectators, mostly Inuit, had attended. The defendants appeared not to understand what was going on, Alikomiak laughing often and at inappropriate times. He was, some argued, probably only sixteen years of age.

Lucas portrayed the killings on the Kent Peninsula as responses to cultural conflict, not reflections of the criminal character of the Inuit. He blamed one of the victims, specifically the trader Otto Binder, and Northern white society generally for destabilizing the traditional society of the Copper Inuit. As he well knew, the traditional society of Inuit in the western Arctic had been ripped pitilessly from its moorings in an extremely short period of time by an insurgence of white traders in search of fur.

Lucas's efforts succeeded in having the hangings postponed. But in the end, he failed to stop them.

In 1924 Knud Rasmussen was travelling westward across Arctic North America on his epic journey known as the Fifth Thule Expedition. In February he was at Tree River. There he learned the story of the hangings of Tatamigana and Alikomiak. He knew of the rapid culture change that was taking place in the western Arctic, and he too was sympathetic. He wrote about the hangings this way:

> Heavy and cumbersome machinery was required to get the two murderers sentenced. Judges, jury and witnesses had to be summoned from long distances. . . .
>
> All that great show of judges, jurymen and witnesses made no particular impression on [the Inuit]; they seemed to be at peace with their conscience. Both were sentenced to death, but first the sentence had to be confirmed by the highest Canadian authorities. Thus it happened that one evening late in winter, while following their customary occupation of making salmon nets, they were informed that they were to be hanged next morning at three o'clock. Young Alikomiak received the news with a smile. The other man, who was somewhat older, felt as if he were choking and

asked for a glass of water. Having taken a drink he too was ready to meet his fate. Just before they were to be executed they gave the wife of the police sergeant some small souvenirs carved in walrus ivory, as a sign that they bore no malice toward the police. They ascended the scaffold with great calmness and met death without fear.

Rasmussen then described the sad fate of the father of one of the two men:

One of the two men had an old father living on Kent Peninsula. When he got to know that at the command of the white man his son had to undertake the long journey to the eternal hunting grounds, he realized that he must not go up there unless someone was there to receive him. This could only be if he killed himself, but the old man was to learn that human life is a tenacious thing. First he tried to shoot himself in the chest with a rifle. When this failed he tried to stab a knife into his heart. As this did not cause death either, he cut his throat and then at last was able to fulfill his self-imposed obligation towards his son.

In early February 1924, Rasmussen took the time to visit the grave of the deceased and wrote sensitively about the powerful emotions he felt there:

It chanced that one winter's day I stood by the old man's grave, which was only protected against wild beasts by one or two simple skins and some blocks of snow. A cold north wind swept over the ground; the drifting snow enveloped me; yet I could not help feeling a stream of warmth through my body, and I had to bow in reverence to the destiny that rested in that lonely grave. Somewhere far away a boy had been hanged by strange men; but on this spot an honourable old heathen had taken his part in expiating the crime by giving his life too.

The Case
of Ikalupiak

A Spirited Defence

In my research on the 1923 trial at Pond Inlet of the three Inuit who were accused of the murder of the Newfoundland fur trader Robert Janes, I concluded that the defence lawyer assigned to defend the Inuit had put forward a very weak case on their behalf. It was indeed fortunate that one of the accused was acquitted and two found guilty of a lesser charge.

What might the outcome have been, I wondered, had they been represented by more aggressive and imaginative counsel?

Then I came across some information on another case, tried in the Mackenzie Delta, in which the accused had more skilful counsel. Unfortunately, not much is known about the case. The year was 1924, and the accused was Ikalupiak.

Ikalupiak was tried for manslaughter in Aklavik for the death of an Inuk whose name was recorded as Mavougach. The crime of which he was accused had occurred far to the east, in the central Arctic, about ninety miles inland from Tree River. The defence counsel, whose surname was McBride and whose first name has not survived in the scanty records I have found, questioned whether Canada even had the jurisdictional authority to try his client. He told the court that Ikalupiak "does not recognize the jurisdiction of this Court. . . . The accused does not consider himself to be a British subject and . . . the law of the white man does not extend to the tribe of one that does not know of their laws."

McBride elaborated: "The instructions which the accused gives to me are that he claims that even if he hurt the deceased Mavougach, the white men have no right to interfere with him. It is his tribe who must hurt or do harm to him." McBride raised other objections, including "that the area included in your Lordship's commission and also these territories do not extend to that part of the territories in which he resides and where the offence occurred."

In requesting a change of venue to the area where the tribe of the accused was located, McBride also raised the subject of why the jury contained no Inuit: "If they [the Eskimos] are British subjects and your Lordship has not called any of the Eskimos here as jurymen, he, the accused, claims that he is in hostile territory as far as these Eskimos are concerned and, therefore, he claims a change of venue to where his tribe is located. . . . And, that, in empanelling the jury, it should include some of his own tribesmen."

In summing up his objections, McBride stated that his client did not "recognize the sovereignty of the Canadian Government and that the white man should not claim sovereignty over his land or his hunting ground. He knows no law but the law of his tribe."

McBride claimed that the objections he raised were "the actual objections in the mind of the accused." If true, Ikalupiak had a fine legal mind and was raising points that would not be heard again in Northern Canada for another half century.

The court nonetheless overruled all of McBride's objections and found Ikalupiak guilty of manslaughter. He was sentenced to five years' incarceration at Stony Mountain Penitentiary in Manitoba.

Thou Shalt Do
No Murder

As a result of the trial of Nuqallaq for the murder of Robert Janes, and other murders in the North that had been brought to the attention of the police and the administration, the Government of Canada decided to overtly inform Inuit of the legal prohibition on murder.

The Department of the Interior had posters prepared in Inuktitut syllabics and English, in parallel texts. The posters measured eighteen inches square and were printed on sailcloth. They were sent north in 1925 and were to be displayed prominently at trading and police posts that Inuit might visit.

The posters were signed by Duncan C. Scott, deputy superintendent of the department from 1923 to 1932, a man whose legacy is controversial, as he believed ardently in the assimilation of Canada's native people. Scott was an enigma—he was one

In Those Days

of Canada's best-known poets, who wrote sensitively about the Canadian landscape and even composed touching poetry about Canada's Aboriginal people, yet as a bureaucrat and an administrator of the country's residential school program, he wrote callously that the government's goal was to "kill the Indian in the child." When informed of the high rates of disease in residential schools, he refused to take any action, saying that this was part of the "final solution of our Indian problem."

Scott's message to Inuit read:

Know Ye.
  The King of the Land commands you, saying:
  "THOU SHALT DO NO MURDER"
  Why does he speak thus?
  Long ago our God made the world, and He owns the world.
  The people also he made, and He owns them.
  The King of the land is commanded by God to protect the people well.
  The white people and Indians and Eskimos have him for their ruler. He is their ruler, therefore he commands, saying:
  "THOU SHALT DO NO MURDER"
  But if a man kills a man, the King sends his servants, the police, to take and kill the murderers.
  But ye do not kill the murderer, nor cause him to be killed. This only the King's servants, the police, ought to do.
  But when a man commits murder, at once tell the King's servants, the police, and he will take and bind the murderer and the ruler will judge him.
  Thus our God commands us so that you are to follow the King's command.

This text was translated into Inuktitut and printed in syllabics; a separate version was published in English and the alphabetic orthography used in western dialects of Inuktitut. One can only wonder what impression this text made on the Inuit reading it. Aside from its white ethnocentrism, it stated boldly and incorrectly that it was the role of the police to seize and kill any Inuit murderers.

One officer, the inspector of the Arctic Sub-District in Aklavik, objected to that very sentiment, complaining to Ottawa that a suspected murderer might resist arrest, feeling that his own life was in jeopardy, and thereby endanger the lives of arresting police. He suggested a change in wording that removed this thought, but not the racism underlying the message as a whole:

"If a man kills a man, the King sends his servants, the Police, to take away the murderer, and bring him before one of the white chiefs, who will hear how the murder was done, and will punish the murderer, if he thinks he is a bad native."

Unfortunately, any reaction Inuit may have had to reading these bizarre posters was never recorded.

The Arctic's Top Cop Commits Suicide

Alfred Herbert Joy had an illustrious career in the Royal Canadian Mounted Police. He joined the force in 1909 at the age of twenty-two. He was a staff sergeant by 1921 and an inspector six years later. Most of his career was spent in the Canadian Arctic, and it is said that from 1914 to 1931 he never spent a summer in the south.

In 1921 Joy went to Pond Inlet to investigate the killing of Robert Janes. He became famous in the High Arctic for his amazing sled patrols. In 1926, from his base at the Craig Harbour detachment, Joy began a series of patrols in the Queen Elizabeth Islands. More than just police patrols, these were also scientific expeditions. Joy mapped and made notes on biology, minerals, archaeology, weather, and ice conditions. His longest dog-sled patrol lasted eighty-one days and covered eighteen hundred miles; he was accompanied by one other constable and a Greenlander employed by the force.

At the end of the 1920s Joy transferred to Montreal, where he was in charge of the Eastern Arctic subdivision. But he continued to travel to the Arctic in the summer on an annual patrol.

Sometime during this period he became engaged to be married to Miss Carmel Murphy of Ottawa. They planned to marry in 1931, but illness intervened; Joy underwent a serious operation, and the marriage had to be postponed.

On Friday, April 29, 1932, the day before his wedding was finally to take place, Joy took the train to Ottawa early in the morning. He checked into the Chateau Laurier Hotel, then went to see a friend before returning to the hotel. He and Carmel had a number of social engagements planned for the day. When she didn't hear from him by noon, she called the hotel. When there was no response to the hotel's page, staff entered his room and found him in bed in a state of semi-consciousness. He was rushed to Ottawa General Hospital, where he died at 7:15 p.m.

The funeral that followed on Monday was one of the largest Ottawa had ever seen.

The procession left the funeral parlour at eight thirty in the morning for St. Theresa's Church, where, two days earlier, Joy should have been married. Reverend Father Leo Lesage, a personal friend who had been scheduled to officiate at the wedding, now conducted his funeral. The newspapers waxed hyperbolic, describing the crowds that lined the streets as "standing bareheaded as the man who conquered the North was following his last trail." The band of the Governor General's Foot Guard played "Nearer My God to Thee."

In Those Days

Joy, who had no relatives in Canada, was interred in the family plot of his fiancée. Nearby stands a large memorial erected later by his father, brothers, and sisters.

The newspaper tributes were effusive: "He was big, powerful, dominant—yet, withal, reticent, kindly, stern and conciliatory as the occasion demanded. He personified the 'strong silent man.'"

One paper reported, "The tribute paid to this gallant adventurer was something more than accorded even to a great statesman or famous soldier. It had about it the glamour of high romance, of a tragically terminated love story, of the sudden and untimely termination of a brilliant career as a knight errant of the Arctic."

In fact, it had more than that. It had a tragic element that the newspapers never reported, if they even knew. Because Alfred Herbert Joy did not die a natural death. He died by his own hand. He had committed suicide alone in his room at the Chateau Laurier Hotel.

I first heard of this suicide in 1978, when I visited the legendary Arctic scientist and explorer J. Dewey Soper. He had known Joy well and had named a mountain north of Lake Harbour (Kimmirut) after him. Soper was staying at the Ford Hotel in Ottawa when Joy died. To him the reasons were simple: The Arctic was in Joy's blood. He couldn't bear the thought of having to sacrifice his freedom to live permanently in the south. And a marriage would chain him there forever. He felt he owed marriage to Carmel, who had waited so long, but he couldn't go through with it. He killed himself.

A northern geologist, Dr. Maurice Haycock, told me a similar story. He had known Joy and, like Soper, had attended his funeral.

The RCMP covered up Joy's suicide. They claim he died of a myocardial infarction—a heart attack—and that is what his death record shows. But there were conflicting reports. The *Ottawa Citizen* reported death from "congestion of the lungs." The *Ottawa Evening Journal* reported the cause as a stroke.

Curious, I tracked down a family member of the late Carmel Murphy through cemetery records. He confirmed the suicide story. He had grown up knowing little about Joy, but thought it odd that someone so famous, and once so close to his own family, was seldom spoken of. Then in 1987, at the funeral of Carmel's sister, an elderly family friend insisted on telling those present about "poor Carmel" and of how her fiancé had killed himself on the day before their wedding.

Carmel never married. She died in 1951, aged forty-nine.

"And the Stars Shall Fall from Heaven"

The Belcher Island Murders

One night in February 1942, a shooting star streaked through the night sky above the Belcher Islands, a remote island group in southern Hudson Bay. Inuit looked heavenward and remembered a Bible verse from Matthew 24: "And the stars shall fall from heaven . . . and they shall see the Son of Man coming in the clouds of heaven with power and great glory."

In the winter of 1940–41, Inuit from the southern group of the Belcher Islands had had vigorous discussions on the meaning of various parts of the Bible. Most of them owned copies of the book printed in the syllabic orthography. They could read the words, but understanding them was another matter. No missionary had ever been resident in the islands, and the Inuit had not had the benefit of any religious instruction. Different Inuit put different interpretations on what they read, and interpreted it in light of the comet they had seen. Some came to the conclusion that the end of the world was near.

Shortly thereafter, nine Inuit would be dead, victims of a religious cult led by two local men, Peter Sala and Charlie Ouyerack, who had proclaimed themselves to be God and Jesus.

Peter Sala was described as "a natural leader" and "one of the best hunters on the Islands." Later reports also described him as being sly and evasive. Ouyerack was described as "a quiet, sickly type of man." Many Inuit prayed to the two self-proclaimed holy men. The RCMP later reported that "some natives destroyed their rifles and dogs, believing that they would have no further use for them due to the imminent end of the world."

But not all Inuit believed in the teachings of the local prophets. Keytoweiack, a lay reader who had perhaps studied the Bible more than the others, was one. So was a young man, Alec Ekpuk, and a sixteen-year-old girl named Sarah Apawkok. On January 25, Sarah was forced to attend a prayer meeting in a snowhouse. When asked if she believed in the teachings of Sala and Ouyerack, she was frightened and said yes. Unfortunately, the others present didn't believe her, and her brother, Alec Apawkok, beat her until she fell unconscious. Ouyerack, asked what should happen to her, said that she should die, whereupon five Inuit dragged her outside, and a young woman only a year older than her beat her to death with a rifle. The next to die was Keytoweiack. The prophets had decided that he was Satan and must die. They ordered Adlaykok to kill him. He dutifully fired two shots through the window of an igloo, killing the man instantly.

In Those Days

Ouyerack then moved his camp to Tukaruk Island, where three other families lived. There he ordered Quarack to kill Alec Ekpuk, who happened to be Quarack's son-in-law, because he did not believe that Ouyerack was Jesus. Quarack obeyed the order, and killed the man with three shots to his body. The RCMP reported that "the natives all rejoiced that Satan was dead."

The death toll up to this time was three. But in early March things escalated, when Peter Sala's sister Mina went mad.

An official report recounted:

On March 9th, whilst Quarack was away hunting and Sala was absent on a trip to Great Whale River . . . Eskimo female Mina, wife of Moses, suddenly became hysterical or insane, and ran to the various igloos in the camp shouting that Jesus was coming to earth and that they must go out to meet Him. Moses . . . and all of the women and children in the camp, with the exception of Quarack's wife, followed Mina out on to the sea ice. Before leaving the shore some of them took off their parkas at Mina's bidding, and Mina and her sister, Kumudluk Sarah, took the parkas off some of the younger children. Mina told them that as Jesus was coming they should meet him in their naked state. She led the party a long way out on to the ice, walking ahead of them, lifting her hands towards the sky and saying, "Come Jesus, Come Jesus." They came to a stop and Kumudluk Sarah persuaded the people to take off their remaining clothing, and to stay there to meet Jesus. These two women helped to undress some of the children. In the meantime, Quarack's wife, who had not been influenced by Mina's mad notion, arrived on the scene and rescued one of her children. Her arrival apparently helped to bring the adult natives to a more rational state of mind, but by this time all of the natives including the children were suffering from frostbite and some were in a state of numbness. Quarack's wife persuaded those who could to put on their clothing and she encouraged them to try to clothe and try to save the others who could not help themselves. Mina returned to camp; her husband, Moses, returned carrying a young boy; Minna, wife of Peter Sala, returned carrying her infant.

Two other women returned to camp, each carrying a child. Two women and four children were too numb to move. They remained on the ice, and froze to death. The two women were Peter Sala and Mina's mother, and their sister, Kumudluk Sarah. Two of the dead children were hers; the other two were the son and stepson of Peter Sala.

Peter Sala was away when the six deaths on the ice occurred. He had travelled to Great Whale River with the Hudson's Bay Company manager Ernie Riddell, who knew nothing of the deaths. While there he told an old company pensioner, whom the Inuit regarded as their "white brother," of the murders of the two men and the teenage girl. The pensioner informed Riddell, who radioed the news out to his headquarters and asked that the police be informed. Sala, Riddell, and a missionary immediately set out for the Belcher Islands. "When they returned Sala learned of the death from exposure of his mother and sister and two children and learned to his sorrow that the religious hysteria in which he had taken a leading part was the cause of their deaths."

It was not until April 11 that the police plane arrived with an investigative team.

In Those Days

The investigation into the Belcher Island murders began on
April 13. It was led by RCMP Corporal W. G. Kerr and assisted by
Dr. T. J. Orford, with Reverend C. Neilsen acting as interpreter.
The bodies of the deceased were examined. Back at the Hudson's
Bay Company post, a coroner's inquiry was held. The Inuit did
not attempt to conceal any of the tragic details of the deaths.

Dr. Orford served a dual role. He was coroner, but also justice
of the peace. In that capacity he charged Mina with murder for
her role in the deaths of the two women and four children. Peter
Quarack was charged with murder in the death of Alec Ekpuk.
Adlaykok was charged with the murder of Keytoweiack, on the
basis of information provided by Peter Sala, who was "evasive
in regard to his part in the murders." The three Inuit thus far
charged were transferred to Moose Factory to await trial. Mina
went "violently insane" there and was transferred to a psychiatric
hospital in Toronto.

In July a police party travelled to the Belcher Islands to continue their investigation and to hold a preliminary hearing. The
three accused were brought back from Moose Factory for this
purpose. The further investigation and examination of the remaining bodies resulted in murder charges being laid against
Peter Sala, Ouyerack, Alec Apawkok, and the young woman
Akeenik. All seven prisoners were committed in custody to
await trial.

While awaiting the arrival of the court party, an influenza
epidemic struck the islands. At one point forty-six Inuit were
down with the flu. One elderly woman died.

The judicial party arrived in the islands on August 18. Judge
Plaxton was from the Ontario Supreme Court, but was also
a stipendiary magistrate for the Northwest Territories. R. A.

Olmsted, from the federal Department of Justice, was the prosecutor. J. P. Madden, a lawyer from Ottawa, was defence counsel. Two reporters, one from the Canadian Press and one from the *Toronto Star*, accompanied the party.

The trial began the following day. The jury consisted of six white men: a mining executive, a prospector, the engineer of the HBC vessel *Fort Charles*, the HBC post manager, and, amazingly, both newspaper reporters. The trial proceeded smoothly for six of the accused. But when it was time for Mina's trial, she refused to leave her tent, and "struggled and screamed and sobbed violently. She had to be carried into Court strapped to a stretcher."

In his address to the jury, the judge noted what he called the Inuit's "easy susceptibility to religious frenzy and hysteria particularly when they were left alone without religious guidance or Police supervision, but pointed out that nevertheless the Criminal laws of Canada were just as applicable to these people as they are to their white brethren."

The jury deliberated for a number of hours before bringing in their verdicts. Alec Apawkok was acquitted. The young lady Akeenik was found not guilty on account of temporary insanity. Peter Sala, Ouyerack, Quarack, and Adlaykok were all found guilty of manslaughter, with strong recommendations for mercy in the cases of Adlaykok and Quarack, the latter because "he was one of the best hunters on the Islands and had the best fed and best clothed family on the Islands, and was ordinarily a quiet man who usually lived and hunted somewhat apart from the other natives and would probably have remained aloof from the religious hysteria had he not been sought out and influenced by the others." In Mina's case, the defence counsel entered no plea, and the jury brought in a verdict that she was insane.

In Those Days

Peter Sala and Ouyerack were sentenced to two years' imprisonment and Adlaykok to one year, all with hard labour, at the RCMP post at Chesterfield Inlet. It was too late in the season for them to be transported to Chesterfield, so they were sent back to Moose Factory, where they, Akeenik, and Mina spent the winter. Quarack was given a two-year suspended sentence and ordered to hunt for, feed, and protect the family of Peter Sala while Sala was imprisoned.

Charlie Ouyerack died at Moose Factory in May of 1942. In the summer of that same year the four remaining prisoners were granted early release on the condition that none return to the Belcher Islands. They were transferred by plane from Moose Factory to Great Whale River. The two women were to be transferred to the care of the Reverend Neilsen, from whom they would receive religious instruction. He, however, had no room to accommodate them, and they were left more or less to fend for themselves.

Peter Sala, his family, and his sister Mina moved to the Nastapoka Islands north of Richmond Gulf. Mina's husband, Moses, drowned in the Belcher Islands in the fall of 1943 before he was able to join her. Adlaykok lived in a camp twenty miles north of Great Whale River. Akeenik lived in the same camp. Quarack remained on the Belcher Islands.

In a brief report in 1944, the RCMP noted that the former prisoners had "been living normal lives and the chief instigators, both while serving imprisonment and since being released and returned to their natural environment have conducted themselves in a normal manner and are now following their normal mode of living."

Peter Sala eventually returned to the Belcher Islands and died there in 1990.

Angulaalik

A Killing at Perry River

ngulaalik was a remarkable Inuk from what is now the Kitikmeot Region of Nunavut. Born about 1898, he lived most of his life in Queen Maud Gulf, southeast of Cambridge Bay.

Captain C. T. Pedersen, an American trader, travelled regularly on his schooner from San Francisco and Seattle into the Kitikmeot to trade with the Inuit. But eventually, as Canadian authority extended northward into what had been a largely lawless land, government authorities informed Pedersen that he must establish a shore base, and that it must be staffed by a Canadian. So Pedersen set up his friend Angulaalik as his resident trader at Perry River in 1928. When Pedersen eventually sold his enterprise to the Hudson's Bay Company, he arranged that Angulaalik would remain as an independent trader, and that the Bay would supply him. At one point Angulaalik had three licensed trading posts.

Angulaalik was a small man, about five feet tall. He proved to be a natural at trading, and lived in a wooden house—a rarity for an Inuk in the Kitikmeot at that time. At Herschel Island he bought a thirty-ton schooner, the *Tudlik*. A soft-hearted missionary had baptized him, even though he had two wives. Sadly, both wives died within a year, and he remarried, to sixteen-year-old Ekvana. On his wedding day, he was re-baptized.

Angulaalik (his name is also spelled *Angulalik*, and he took the first name Stephen) was much written about. Articles and photographs of the Inuit trader were published worldwide. He was awarded the King George V Silver Jubilee Medal in 1935, and the Queen's Coronation Medal in 1953 for "outstanding leadership." He was also unique in the region in owning a camera—a number of his photographs are preserved in the Prince of Wales Heritage Centre in Yellowknife.

Duncan Pryde, a trader who worked with Angulaalik in 1961, described him as "a small man with a charming smile, the kind of smile that flashes from a toothpaste advertisement" and "a fine trapper and hunter, a man of very strong will, which he easily imposed on the other Eskimos, a man accustomed to having things his own way." He was "strong for his stature, but basically he seemed a gentle man."

Amazingly, considering his success as a trader and the skills one would think would be a prerequisite for that success, Angulaalik was illiterate in both English and Inuktitut. The scholar Robin McGrath wrote, "Virtually alone among all the other Inuit, he could not read or write Inuktitut." And yet he had a typewriter and often typed his orders to the HBC supply centre in

Edmonton—he simply copied brand names from the packages. Sometimes he got it wrong. His occasional mistakes caused considerable mirth at the depot when he would order "24 Keep in Cool Place" or "10 Made in England."

With success came jealousy and enemies. One was Utuittuq (official records spell his name *Otoetok*), a local bully whose like-minded sons were in the habit of pilfering goods from Angulaalik's store. When they were caught and forced to return stolen items, their father was angry and humiliated. His dislike of Angulaalik intensified, and he often threatened him and told others that someday he would kill him.

On New Year's Eve, 1956, Angulaalik and Utuittuq both attended a party at Norman Eevalik's house, a party featuring four pots of homebrew. Everyone there was drunk. The two rivals got into an altercation, and Utuittuq pushed Angulaalik around the crowded room. Angulaalik may have panicked. He took a small knife from his belt and "poked" Utuittuq. Despite the bulky jacket he was wearing, Utuittuq suffered a small cut on the arm and a wound to his abdomen. He left and spent the rest of the evening visiting others who were not at the party, feasting on caribou meat and drinking copious quantities of tea. He would raise his parka to show his hosts the small wound to his stomach, apparently proud of having caused Angulaalik to lose his temper.

On January 4, Utuittuq died from the small wound to his abdomen, his death the result of a "strangulated bowel." The doctor who later performed an autopsy testified that his life could have been saved with elementary first aid, even the simple act of placing adhesive over the wound and enjoying some bedrest.

Angulaalik dictated a letter of confession to Norman Eevalik, host of the fatal party, who wrote it down in Inuktitut. He dispatched two copies with a messenger by sled to Cambridge Bay, one to the police and one to the HBC trader. At Cambridge Bay, it was translated into very rough English by George Washington Porter, son of an Inuk woman and a white father, the whaler W. P. S. Porter (sometimes known as "Alphabetical Porter" because of his many initials).

The translation read:

I say a few words to the police. I got scared of man and ran away from him. Since long he been go after me. How I get mad with him Otoetok. I don't want to kill him. I couldn't help it. With a knife. In a party and drinking. And I poked him. He go after me and I couldn't help it. People. Happy amongs [sic] them. Lots of people. Lots of them. They are fighting among them. He caught me and I poked him. In Norman's house. I was drunk. After that for myself when he died, when I got sober, I like to kill myself. I was thinking about my family. Got nobody to watch for them and nobody to keep them. I don't know that when he go after me. I got scared of him. I don't want to do anything bad for the people. He been bothering me. He been go after me. Since a long time. He go after me and I got scared of him. I did it.

As Robin McGrath has written, Angulaalik was fluent in several Inuit dialects and was an eloquent speaker. This pidgin English translation may have conveyed an erroneous impression to the authorities that Angulaalik was an unsophisticated man.

When Angulaalik's family provided McGrath with a carbon

copy of Angulaalik's original letter, she was appalled at the sloppy translation job that had been done for the police in 1957. She asked competent interpreters who worked in the legislature in Yellowknife to retranslate it. The result is a more lucid rendition of the man's thoughts at the time of writing:

> I want to say a few things to the police. I was afraid and never thought of the consequences. For a long time Otoetok was after me; finally I got angry. I did not intend to kill him, but he kept after me and during a drinking party I poked him with a cutting knife because he kept bothering me. People were partying in Norman Eevalik's house; in the middle of all the people we were wrestling and it was there I poked him while I was drunk. The day after he died, when I sobered up, I thought of committing suicide, but I didn't because I have children. I thought of my children and how they have no one else to support them. This is my confession. I was afraid of him; I never bother anyone normally, but one person kept mocking me. Otoetok was following me all the time and I began to be afraid so I poked him.

Corporal Edward Jones and Special Constable Jimmy Nahagao-oloak travelled to Perry River to investigate the events. Angulaalik received them on their arrival and fed them. He provided a verbal statement in Inuktitut, interpreted by the special constable and written down by Jones. The officer then charged him with murder.

The case came to trial in Cambridge Bay in May 1957. Judge John Howard Sissons officiated.

Sissons had practiced law in Alberta before he was appointed as the first judge of the Territorial Court of the Northwest Territories in 1955. He took the court on the road, believing that the accused should be tried as close as possible to where the crime was committed. As a result, it was estimated that Sissons travelled 275,000 miles by plane and dog sled to preside over trials in the North.

Sissons had already made groundbreaking decisions regarding Inuit custom marriage and adoption, hunting and liquor infractions, and murder. Many of those decisions had enraged the government of the time—their agenda was clearly one of rapid acculturation of native people. But Sissons had a different agenda. In the words of a writer commenting after his retirement, he "merged a profound reverence for ancient legal tradition with a unique ability to adapt those traditions to the challenges of new situations. In his eyes, the law did not exist above society, but within society: it must be tested and retested against the demands that society made upon it."

Sissons would not admit into evidence Angulaalik's statement to Corporal Jones, ruling that "it could not be established that the statement reported by the corporal was what Angulaalik said or meant." Neither did he admit the letter of confession, writing that "Angulaalik had not written this letter. He had asked his host at the fatal party, Norman Eevalik, to write it for him and he could not read what Norman had written. It was perfectly proper for the Hudson's Bay Company to guess what was meant by 'two cases of fragile' or 'three dozen handle with care,' and to presume further that the order was voluntary. But our courts cannot guess."

The trial was by jury, but it was hardly by a group of Angulaalik's peers. All the jurors were white. Nonetheless, they brought in a verdict of not guilty. Angulaalik was acquitted.

Tragically, at a party thrown that night to celebrate the acquittal, homebrew reared its ugly head again. This time it was laced with methyl hydrate. Two people died.

When Angulaalik was arrested and taken to Cambridge Bay to await trial, he may have anticipated a long incarceration, for he formally turned over his store to the HBC. He never got it back. On his return to Perry River, he was no longer the man in charge. He endured the humiliation of becoming the post servant, subservient to the orders of a white manager. One of those managers, Duncan Pryde, wrote in his best-selling book *Nunaga* that Angulaalik had committed a number of other unreported murders. If true, the police never heard about them, and no one else has ever documented this allegation.

In 1967 Angulaalik and Ekvana moved to Cambridge Bay so their children could go to school. But they returned each summer to Perry River. Angulaalik, once a very successful Inuit businessman, passed away in 1980.

Isaac Shooyook, MLA, and the Killing of Soosee

In the fall of 2013, Isaac Shooyook of Arctic Bay made history by becoming the oldest person elected to the Nunavut legislature in its fourteen-year history. He was seventy-four. But when one thinks of Isaac Shooyook, *old* is not a word that comes easily to mind. For Shooyook is not *old*, but rather *timeless*. *Resilient* and *gentle* are adjectives that also suggest themselves. And making history is nothing new for this quiet, unassuming man.

In 1965 Isaac Shooyook was a young hunter of twenty-six living in a traditional camp at Fort Ross on the Boothia Peninsula. A former Hudson's Bay Company trading post, Fort Ross had been closed in 1947 because it had proven too difficult for the company to resupply. Inuit in the area then traded into Spence

Bay (now Taloyoak). By the mid-1960s, at a time when many Inuit had already moved into larger communities where the government provided housing, education, and medical services, this camp of about twenty people, under the leadership of Napatchee-Kadluk, was extremely isolated.

Napatchee-Kadluk's wife, Soosee, was mentally ill; she suffered from paranoid schizophrenia. She had spent two periods of time in hospital in Edmonton, but each time she returned, uncured, to her traditional camp and her family. When in the grip of her madness, Soosee was dangerous to her family and campmates. She would threaten to kill people, and blow her breath on them, and they feared that this would transmit her illness to them. She was a large woman, and strong. At times she destroyed some of the camp's equipment, damaging boats and other items that were crucial to the survival of a hunting community.

In July 1965 the situation became critical. We know of the state of fear in the community largely because one of the camp leaders—Shooyook's father, Kadlu, who was Napatchee-Kadluk's brother-in-law—kept a detailed diary of the events. His observations are heart-rending. On July 9 he wrote:

"She's throwing things out of the tent, and she hasn't been sleeping for a while. . . . She's throwing rocks, and pulling her hair out. It looks as if she's going to kill her husband, and she's throwing rocks at us all, and blowing her breath. We love her but we have to tie her up."

Napatchee-Kadluk decided that everyone except Soosee and him would relocate to a small island nearby, close enough that they could observe her behaviour. He would remain in the camp with his wife. But Kadlu dissuaded him from staying. In the end everyone but Soosee left the camp, but not before they had bound her tightly with ropes. From the safety of the island, they watched her through their telescopes. And they saw her break her bonds with superhuman force.

"During today she has knocked over all the tents," wrote Kadlu. "She's breaking up all the gear. We are watching her doing this. . . . We had to leave our gear, and now she is breaking it all up. She wants to kill us. . . . The devil is making her do these things. . . . We are praying to God in Heaven to help us."

Soosee was not getting any better. And so Napatchee-Kadluk and Kadlu conferred. Kadlu, of course, recorded their decision in his detailed diary:

"We are certain that the devil is making her do these things. The only thing to do now is for someone to go after her. If she runs away she will not be hurt, and they will not do anything to her. If she comes after them she will be shot, because we are really afraid of her, because she has been saying that she is going to kill everyone."

Shooyook and his cousin, Soosee's son Aiyoot, were dispatched to the camp with Shooyook's brother Naketakvek and one other man. Shooyook and Aiyoot were instructed to take the necessary but regrettable action.

Naketakvek recalled later what happened when the party reached the beach: "When Soosee saw them she started to come towards them. A number of shots were fired to warn her away, but she kept coming. . . . When the bullets were flying around her she just kept on coming towards them. She was blowing in their faces."

Shooyook ran out of ammunition. He took Aiyoot's gun and fired the shots that killed his aunt, Aiyoot's mother.

Their campmates, watching from the island, knelt in prayer

and gave thanks to God. As Kadlu noted, He had helped them to triumph. They returned to camp and buried Soosee shortly thereafter.

That fall a plane arrived to take the camp children to far-off Aklavik for school. The plane also carried Kadlu's account of the tragedy to the RCMP.

The Inuit at Fort Ross did not try to hide what they had done from the authorities. On the contrary, they reported the act themselves. The killing of Soosee had been a necessity, a decision taken as a last resort to preserve their own lives.

The subsequent trial of Shooyook and Aiyoot for murder was the first trial by jury held in Spence Bay. David Searle, a prominent Yellowknife lawyer, was the prosecutor. Aiyoot's lawyer was Howard Irving. William Morrow acted for Shooyook.

The presiding judge was John Howard Sissons. A remarkable man who often rendered precedent-setting judgments, he was the first judge of the Territorial Court of the Northwest Territories. Sissons was seventy-three years old when he presided over the trial of Shooyook and Aiyoot. This would be his last case before retirement, and would cause *Maclean's* magazine to choose him as one of the outstanding Canadians of 1966, describing him as "the angry old man in a hurry."

In his opening remarks to the jury, David Searle acknowledged the difficulty of this case. Describing the crime scene, he said, "There is no RCMP detachment there, no Northern Affairs Officer, no nursing station, and no Hudson's Bay Company post. . . . Our sympathy must be with these people who found themselves in this impossible situation."

Kadlu was called as first witness. When asked if they could not have taken Soosee to Spence Bay and turned her over to the authorities there, he pointed out that they could have done that if it had been winter, but in early July, no, there was too much ice for boat travel but not enough for sled travel, and the rivers were already running. "We knew the police would not like this," he said, "but she would have killed a lot of people. That's the reason why we killed her."

William Morrow, in defence of Shooyook, pointed out that Soosee could have killed someone at any moment: "You could have had the same situation anywhere else in North America, but you had it here in Fort Ross. You had it under the circumstances where you had no remedy, no way to clear it up, and what happened was the justifiable result." Morrow urged the jury to bring in a verdict of not guilty.

The jury of six members—all that were required at the time—included a woman, the first female juror in the North, and two Inuit. They did not find their task easy. Delores Koening, the woman juror, spoke later about some of the deliberations the jurors had had behind closed doors:

"They [the Inuit] felt very differently from the way the legal people felt. They said, 'They killed a woman and therefore they are guilty.' But then when we said according to Canadian law if you are guilty of first degree murder you should be hung. . . they said, 'Well, no, they shouldn't be hung. They killed her but they shouldn't be hung.' So that was what the debate was about."

The debate, in fact, centred around the legal meanings of the far-from-simple terms "guilty" and "not guilty." The Inuit of the time, in a courtroom setting that, despite the best interests and intentions of Judge Sissons, was a foreign and intimidating place, understood these terms, simplistically, as meaning "Did they do it?" or "Did they not do it?" A better understanding—which, however, took many years to evolve in the Northern court system —would have been something like, "Do they (or do they not) deserve to bear blame for what they did?"

In the end, the jury acquitted Aiyoot, and convicted Shooyook of the lesser charge of manslaughter, with a strong recommendation for clemency. Sissons gave him a two-year suspended sentence.

William Morrow, who succeeded Sissons as judge of the territorial court, called this "a great social verdict" and "a complete vindication of the jury system." He commented, "A judge trying the case alone would have had to find both men guilty in law, and what a travesty that would have been. But the jury saved the day. In its absolute power, it could ignore the law, as it did, and bring in a socially acceptable verdict."

Isaac Shooyook returned from his trial in Spence Bay to his camp near Fort Ross. But camp life was dying. Not long thereafter, Kadlu and his family, which included sons Shooyook and Naketakvek, moved to Arctic Bay. Shooyook was one of many who combined hunting and wage labour to build a stable life for his family. He is a community elder, a devout churchgoer, a quiet and stable resource for his community. He made legal history in 1966. He made history again in 2013 when, at the age of seventy-four, he became the oldest person to be elected to the Nunavut legislature. But, as I said at the beginning, Isaac Shooyook is not old. Rather, he is timeless.

Death on an Ice Island

T3 was an ice island seven miles long and three miles wide, drifting in the Arctic Ocean when twenty researchers arrived there in May 1970. They were from the United States Weather Bureau and were to remain for five months. The atmosphere was cozy, despite the sometimes minus-sixty-degree outdoor temperature—the men lived in trailers and worked in well-insulated research huts. Supply by cargo aircraft in the spring was not a problem; the ice island had probably broken off from Ellesmere Island over three decades earlier, and was made of freshwater ice about 130 feet thick. It had first been occupied by researchers in 1952. In addition to its official name, T3, it was also known as Fletcher's Ice Island.

One of the researchers was Donald Leavitt. His nickname was Porky. And Porky had a drinking problem. Booze was scarce on their drifting home, and expensive—those who ordered it had to pay for it themselves. Many found ingredients in the mess and simply made homebrew. On three occasions in the first two months on the island, when Porky had finished his own supply, he threatened his campmates with a meat cleaver in order to steal theirs.

On July 7 Porky stole a bottle of homemade raisin wine from Mario Escamilla's room. He and his friend Bennie Lightsy, nominally the station manager, were drinking it, mixed with ethyl alcohol, when Escamilla's friend Charles Parodi arrived with a rifle and retrieved what was left of his friend's wine.

After Escamilla got off work and went back to his trailer, he found the loaded rifle that Parodi had left there. He had it in his hands when Lightsy—still tipsy—arrived and began to argue with him over his selfishness in not sharing his wine. Escamilla accidentally bumped the rifle against something during this animated discussion. It went off, killing Lightsy.

This killing on an ice island presented a potential legal conundrum. T3 did not legally belong to any nation. Usually, but not always, it drifted in the Canadian portion of the Arctic Ocean, but all the personnel were Americans. And international law held that an accused should be tried in the district where he committed his crime, or where he was first brought after committing his crime. Mario Escamilla would be charged. But where should he be tried?

The answer depended in part on the quick thinking of government officials in the United States. The last cargo flight to T3 had been on June 8. After that date, there would be no more aircraft arriving for three months, because the spring weather in the High Arctic meant that the sometime landing surface was too slushy for a safe arrival. Escamilla would have to be airlifted out by helicopter. At that time, T3 was three hundred miles from the North Pole, almost midway between the pole and the Canadian military base at Alert on the northern tip of Ellesmere Island. A military helicopter from the American base at Thule, Greenland, could be dispatched, and it could refuel on the way north at Alert. But once Escamilla was on board, the chopper could not land there for fuel on its return journey—if he set foot in Canada, then Canada would have jurisdiction. And the chopper did not have enough range to return to Thule without refuelling.

This logistical nightmare was solved—with great difficulty— by having the chopper, an HH-3E helicopter known as the Jolly Green Giant, refuelled in the air by an American C-130 Hercules tanker. The chopper safely reached the American base at Thule, Greenland, from where Escamilla continued on to the United States in a military transport.

Canada made the prosecution of Escamilla easier when it officially waived jurisdiction over this specific incident "without prejudice to a possible future claim of jurisdiction over T-3." An American report at the time notes, "Canada has previously argued that it has territorial sovereignty over all Arctic islands to the North Pole. Pierre Trudeau, the current Prime Minister of Canada, however, recently expressed the opinion that this sovereignty does not apply to water and ice. The reason for waiv- ing jurisdiction over the T-3 case was a desire not to interfere with the course of justice for the sake of clarifying a very complex point of international law." (I am sure that Canada would take a very different position were a similar case to arise today.)

Most controversially, the United States decided that the

floating ice island was legally a US vessel—the same as a ship—and so the case would be tried under US marine law.

Escamilla was lucky. The rifle he had used was proven to be defective—it would fire if it was bumped against something solid, even with no finger on the trigger. The jury found Escamilla guilty of involuntary manslaughter and sentenced him to three years. He served sixty days before his appeal was heard. He never returned to jail.

T3 continued its vagrant voyage through northern waters and finally broke up off the coast of Greenland in 1984.

Acknowledgements

All of the stories contained in this volume were originally published in the author's column Taissumani in *Nunatsiaq News*. Original titles and publication dates are as follows:

"A Hostage-Taking in the Arctic" originally appeared as "A Fifteenth-Century Hostage-Taking in the Arctic" on August 3, 2007.

"Five Missing Men" originally appeared as "Five Missing Men" on August 10, 2007.

"Henry Hudson's Mutineers and the Inuit" originally appeared as "Hudson's Mutineers and the Inuit" and "The Knife" on January 18 and January 25, 2008.

"Massacre at Knapp's Bay" originally appeared as "Massacre at Knapp's Bay" on July 21, 2006.

"Slaughter at Bloody Fall" originally appeared as "Slaughter at Bloody Fall" on July 15, 2005.

In Those Days

"Robert Hood: Passion and Murder in the North" originally appeared as "Robert Hood — Passion and Murder in the Arctic" on January 2, 2015.

"Inuit Evidence in a British Court" originally appeared as "Inuit Evidence in a British Court — Part One" and "Inuit Evidence in a British Court — Part Two" on February 15 and February 22, 2008.

"Murder at Repulse Bay" originally appeared as "Murder at Repulse Bay — Part One" and "Murder at Repulse Bay — Part Two" on September 7 and September 14, 2007.

"How Do You Spell Murder? The Death of Charles Francis Hall" originally appeared as "How Do You Spell Murder? — The Death of Charles Francis Hall" and "Who Killed Charles Francis Hall?" on November 14 and November 21, 2014.

"The Execution of Private Henry" originally appeared as "The Execution of Private Henry" on June 3, 2005.

"The Killing of Ross Marvin" originally appeared as "The Killing of Ross Marvin" on April 8, 2005.

"Christian Klengenberg: An Arctic Enigma" originally appeared as "Christian Klengenberg: An Arctic Enigma"; "Christian Klengenberg — More Suspicions"; and "Christian Klengenberg — The Rest of the Story" on February 27, March 6, and March 13, 2009.

"Can a Man Be Mistaken for a Seal?" originally appeared as "Can a Man Be Mistaken for a Seal?" on May 2, 2008.

"The Killing of Radford and Street" originally appeared as "The Killing of Radford and Street — Part One" and "The Killing of Radford and Street — Part Two" on October 8 and October 15, 2010.

Collected Writings on Arctic History

"Sinnisiak and Uluksuk" originally appeared as "Sinnisiak and Uluksuk, Part One"; "Sinnisiak and Uluksuk, Part Two"; "Sinnisiak and Uluksuk, Part Three"; and "Sinnisiak and Uluksuk, Part Four" on January 7, January 14, January 21, and January 28, 2011.

"Getting Away with Murder" originally appeared as "Getting Away with Murder" on April 28, 2006.

"Blood on the Snow: Robert Janes's Last Journey" originally appeared as "Escape from the Arctic — Robert Janes's Last Journey"; "Away Goes February — Robert Janes's Last Journey"; "Arrival at Cape Crauford — Robert Janes's Last Journey"; and "Blood on the Snow — Robert Janes's Last Journey" on February 18, February 25, March 4, and March 11, 2005.

"The Trial and Punishment of Nuqallaq" originally appeared as "A Circus of Formality"; "The Trial of Nuqallaq Begins"; and "Nuqallaq Returns to Pond Inlet" on February 4, 2005, August 25, 2006, and September 1, 2006.

"Deputizing a Murderer" originally appeared as "A Murderer is Deputized as Special Constable of the RCMP" on April 7, 2006.

"The Only Inuit Hanged in Canada" originally appeared as "The Only Hanging of Inuit in Canada" and "More on the Herschel Island Hangings" on January 27 and February 3, 2006.

"The Case of Ikalupiak: A Spirited Defence" originally appeared as "The Case of Ikalupiak, a Spirited Defence" on November 13, 2009.

"Thou Shalt Do No Murder" originally appeared as "Thou Shalt Do No Murder" on November 1, 2013.

"The Arctic's Top Cop Commits Suicide" originally appeared as "The Arctic's Top Cop Commits Suicide" on April 29, 2005.

In Those Days

"'And the Stars Shall Fall from Heaven": The Belcher Island Murders" originally appeared as "'And the Stars Shall Fall from Heaven'— The Belcher Island Murders"; "The Belcher Island Murders — Part Two"; and "The Belcher Island Murders — Part Three" on December 5, December 12, and December 19, 2014.

"Angulaalik: A Killing at Perry River" originally appeared as "Angulaalik: A Killing at Perry River — Part One" and "Angulaalik: A Killing at Perry River — Part Two" on January 9 and January 16, 2015.

"Isaac Shooyook, MLA, and the Killing of Soosee" originally appeared as "Isaac Shooyook, MLA — The Tragic Events of 1965" and "Isaac Shooyook on Trial" on March 21 and March 28, 2014.

"Death on an Ice Island" originally appeared as "Death on an Ice Island" on November 28, 2014.